Finding Faith

Lessons Uncovered Through the Storms

Indiana Tuggle

VICTORY
PUBLISHING INC

Copyright © 2018 by Indiana Tuggle. All rights reserved.

Victory Publishing CO
PO Box 752384
Memphis, TN 38175

Front Cover, Art and Full wrap designed by Kanika Harris

Author photograph taken by Patrick C Covington Photography

Edited by Kat Spencer

All rights reserved solely by the author. The author guarantees all content is original and does not infringe upon the legal rights of any other person or work. No part of this book may be reproduced in any form–except for brief quotations in print reviews, without prior permission of the author.
Unless otherwise indicated, Scripture quotations are taken from the Holy Bible, New King James Version (NKJV) @ 1979, 1980, 1982, 1990 by Thomas Nelson Inc.

ISBN 13: 978-0-9993411-6-2

LCCN: 2018909537

Printed in the United States of America

DEDICATION

This book is dedicated to those struggling to understand the various trials and tribulations life has thrown or is throwing their way.

May you be encouraged to grow closer in your walk with Christ and strengthened to stand on His never-failing word and promises.

TABLE OF CONTENTS

i	Introduction
1	Chapter One: Yes You
11	Chapter Two: When God Stops Talking
23	Chapter Three: If Only You Believed
39	Chapter Four: Fear of the Unknown
51	Chapter Five: Are You Ready for What You Asked for?
67	Chapter Six: Surrender
81	Chapter Seven: In the Shadow of the Almighty
97	Chapter Eight: When Mourning Comes
111	Chapter Nine: New Beginnings
123	Chapter Ten: What You Said
138	About the Author
141	Acknowledgements
143	A Word from the Author

INTRODUCTION

Just have faith!

How many times have you heard this phrase? If you had a nickel for every time you've heard it you'd be rich, right? Well hopefully not, because if you are like me, the words seem to slide off the lips of sister, brother, mother or pastor so and so at the most inopportune time. Your life was taking a sky dive off Mt. Everest. The moment those words hit your ear drum, they instantly sent instructions to your eyes to roll and your feet to walk away quickly, because if your mouth had a chance to respond it wasn't going to be pretty!

You weren't really mad at sister, brother, mother or pastor so and so, you were just frustrated. "Just have faith" implied that you were not doing anything or that whatever you were doing was completely wrong! Truth is, faith wasn't your problem (so you think). Your problem was trying to understand when! When was God going to bring you out? When was God going to turn things around for your good? When was He going to make your enemies your footstool? When was your break through, miracle, and blessing coming? You were tired of hearing "Just have faith" because those words meant that your time of suffering was not over!

I left my job of fifteen years in 2013. I wanted to help people in poverty gain control of their lives and create a plan of success. It was my passion and my past. I made it, so it was my duty to help others make it too. I knew I heard God say, "Trust me," when I froze at the proposed salary which was $5000 less than I was making, so I leaped at the opportunity, saying goodbye to fear and taking faith by the hand. Just a short eighteen months later, that company lost its government contract. Myself and 400+ employees across the state found ourselves unemployed. I had been working since I was 17 and this was the first time I had ever been without work!

At first, I was excited as I had ideas of starting my own business, but as the days turned into months, and the months into a year, I began to question whether I heard God correctly, whether I understood my purpose or whether it was God I heard at all! I knew the word. I wrote down every promise God had spoken over me through others and meditated on them often. Yet where was my faith?

Finding Faith is a look back over the things I experienced and the revelation of what faith looks like as well as how those experiences gave me the strength and courage to plow forward. Faith is best understood looking back. The journey backward helped me understand why God allowed certain things to happen and how trusting Him allowed Him to turn them around for not only my good but to help others. Finding Faith is for those who are struggling to understand why God allows bad things to happen to good people or why pain and hurt is even necessary.

In reading Finding Faith, it is my hope that it sparks a willingness to look back over your own experiences and find strength and joy, not in going through but in making it out. For it is the revelation of how you made it out that you will find your faith and uncover the true love of Christ.

CHAPTER ONE

Yes You

Pain is the dirt required to nurture and awaken the seed of faith within. Faith uncovers the victory in making it out rather than the pain of going through.

If we really knew what we had to, or shall I say, needed to go through to get to the promises of God, would we choose to go anyway? If we knew what greatness, prosperity, and success would cost us, would we pursue it anyway? If we knew the sacrifices we would make, the things and people we would lose, or the tears we would shed, would we ask for it anyway? If the children of Israel knew that they would wander in the wilderness for forty years, would they have rather remained in captivity? Well, we know from the story, that the complaining and regrets started at the first sign of trouble . . . the Red Sea!

I now understand why God never shows us the journey. Truth be told, He really never shows us the end. The sacrifices to obtain freedom are great, but the benefits are even greater. Life is abundantly better than and more than we could even imagine. Our dreams and goals are mere fragments of what God has in store. Our visions are mere glimpses of the benefits of loving, trusting and having faith in God.

But even when you know, that you know, that you know what God created you for and what He has promised you, when the testing comes it hits like an 18-wheeler!

Why Me?

By the age of 18 life had dealt me a hand no child should be subjected to. Life molested me, abused me, and left me in poverty searching for love. I saw little boys forced to be men sucked into a life of drugs and crime to put food on the table and care for drug addicted mothers. I saw little girls using their bodies for cheap clothes, a happy meal, and a movie. I saw grown women subjecting themselves to emotional and physical abuse for a title of "ride or die chic," "girlfriend," or "boo-thang." I watched little girls trade books for babies. I watched mothers encourage their daughters to have babies to obtain welfare and food stamps to help out around the house. I saw mothers sell their daughters to drug dealers for a quick high or a few dollars. I saw men treat women as truck stops, moving from one to another with the rising and setting of the sun. I saw men watching these women fight over them with no intervention only to continue seeing and sleeping with them all.

I once thought that it would have been easier to succumb to the environment and just go with the flow. I tried skipping school, smoking marijuana, and hanging with the "fast" girls to fit in. Though I skipped school my grades didn't slack, and I therefore managed to stay under my mom's radar. I even tried to get pregnant. My boyfriend and I had sex EVERY day, sometimes three to four times a day. I didn't get pregnant, but

Finding Faith

I did get Chlamydia . . . guess he wasn't in love as much as he said. I found out that while he was my one and only, I was one of many to him. I was in love though, he was my first everything. First to call me pretty, first to want me, he saved me... so I thought.

Before him, after the molestations, things were rough for me. I felt ugly and fat. I still didn't fit in, though I tried. I was still the quiet girl, the good girl, and the one popular girls avoided. I was the butt of every fat joke. I was made fun of for being smart. The girls I hung with just did so because I was nice. They were the bad girls; the boys were in and out of their house, they were popular and I wanted to be just like them. But the boys didn't like me, so I sat in the house and observed. One day I couldn't take the loneliness anymore and took a knife to my wrist. I didn't really want to die, I just wanted somebody to notice me. I felt invisible. I felt ugly. I felt worthless. When I met him, he told me I was pretty and he wanted to be with me. I was fourteen, way too young for sex, but according to my new friends, I was the only one still a virgin. So, I did it anyway, only to discover later, I was actually the first one in the group to have sex.

My teenage years and high school years were no walk in the park. The projects, where I lived, was not Mr. Roger's neighborhood. While most who lived there remember great stories, great people and a sense of familial bonding. I remember pain, loneliness, and abuse. By eighteen, though graduating 4th in my class with a 3.5 GPA, I was not concerned with college, I just wanted out. I remember asking God, "There must be something better?" It took me a long time to figure out exactly what I wanted to do with my life. But leaving the projects took me into unchartered territory. I formed real friendships, found a good job, went back to school and bought a house. Most importantly I went back to church.

My first encounter with God, beyond the 'prayer of salvation,' was eye opening. My church home taught me how to build a relationship with God. I began to read the bible and pray on my own, and God began to talk back. I was excited and began to share what He would reveal. God began to show me that He was with me all along. He is the reason why I never fit in. He is the reason why I didn't lose my mind though I was molested several times. He is the reason I didn't get pregnant, though I tried extremely hard. The men I thought I loved and loved me, were sent by the enemy to stop God's plan. Had I reproduced with them I would have ended up like the women and girls I grew up with. My issues with my pre-menstrual cycle and polycystic ovaries were blessings in disguise that prevented me from becoming a mother too soon.

When things in life knock us down, we are quick to proclaim, "Why Me?" "Why not you?" says God. "It's not about you." If I had never been through those terrible teenage years, could I be credible in telling others that they could get beyond poverty and sexual abuse? If I had never gotten a degree, could I tell others that education is the key to success? If I had never been bullied or felt worthless, could I tell others that self-love is possible? Many people say that you don't have to touch fire to know that it burns . . . which is true. But if you have never been burned, how do you know what it takes to heal? People who are hurting respond to people who can relate to their hurt.

It's not about you. Somebody has to be the first. Somebody has to have the courage to go through so they can teach others how to get through. Somebody has to teach those who can't avoid the fire, how to handle the heat and heal the burn. Your purpose is discovered in two areas: 1. your pain and/or 2. your knowledge. What hurt are you holding on to? The final act of forgiveness and moving on is recognizing that your hurt can be used to help others.

No temptation has overtaken you except such as is common to man; but God is faithful, who will not allow you to be tempted beyond what you are able, but with the temptation will also make the way of escape, that you may be able to bear it.

—1 Corinthians 10:13 (NKJV)

The first thing the enemy wants us to think, when we have gone through something or are currently going through something, is that we are alone. Your past could be that "way of escape" for someone else. You may be the one God sent, so that they are "able to bear it." God's faithfulness will not allow Him to turn a deaf ear to His people. We are God in the Earth, what you have been through, was not just for you, it is for others so that God will be glorified.

What do you know that can be used to help someone else?

My people are destroyed for lack of knowledge. Because you have rejected knowledge, I also will reject you from being priest for Me; because you have forgotten the law of your God, I also will forget your children.

—Hosea 4:6 (NKJV)

Don't assume that people have access to the same knowledge or education as you. Just because you are of the same race, same gender, same background, same etc., does not mean that you share the same knowledge. The bible tells us that the mystery of the kingdom is given to us but is hidden from the world.

As Christians, as His disciples we are compelled to share this knowledge. This is the great commission, this is the good news we are to spread throughout the earth.

Earthly knowledge, or text book knowledge, is available to all. Life's experiences, trials and tribulations, will happen to us all. But it is the knowledge of God that allows us to navigate through a sinful world. Happiness is available but it is not automatic. We must choose to be happy and pursue it diligently. The world is desperately crying out for the peace of God. This peace is only found in His presence. Pain and turmoil are sent to delay happiness. Without God to show us how to stand in the face of the enemy, the pain and turmoil can overtake us and cause us to dwell in a life of existence rather than abundance.

"Why me?" you ask. Our experiences unite us. In order for what the devil meant for evil to be used for good, we have to give it over to God. How do we give it over to God?

1. Recognize the omnipresence of God. Though it was hard, painful and brought you to your knees, recognize that God was with you and He is the reason you made it through.

2. Recognize you are blessed. You came through with your right mind. If you do the

> *The foundation of faith is in the knowledge and character of God. The knowledge that God is able to deliver, that God is our provider, that God is a healer, and that He is all that we need Him to be, is not known to all.*

research of others in your same situation, you will see that your ability to come out on the other side is unique. Stop allowing the enemy to tell you that you are not special.

3. Recognize God's strength and power. The enemy cannot give life, nor can he take it away. He must have God's permission. The fact that God did not allow the enemy to kill you, means your purpose is greater than your pain.

4. Acknowledge your feelings and stop living in regret. The situation was painful and you have the right to be hurt. Forgive others, forgive yourself and let it go. Look back with gratitude rather than regret. As painful as it was, it taught you valuable lessons and helped sculpt you into the person you are today. If you don't like the person you are today, it is because you are still living in regret and need God's forgiveness. Remember true forgiveness is: letting go of what if (the hope of a different past). You can't go back, you can't change it.

5. Recognize that others need you. If you are willing to be transparent, what you went through can help others. People are hurting and your transparency will draw them to you. Many say, people like drama. Drama is familiar. All have been hurt and can relate to the hurt of others. But we must show them that God wants to heal the hurt and show them a life of abundance. Drama cannot be avoided but we can go through it and not allow the same drama to impact every area of our lives.

Are you still wondering why me? Please recognize that the constant asking of this question prolongs the pain. Research shows that the children of Israel wandered in the wilderness 40 years for what should have been an eleven-day journey. How in the world did they make 11 days last 40 years? Murmuring and complaining, that's how. They didn't recognize they were going around the same mountain.

God was so upset at the complaints, doubt and lack of faith that He proclaimed that generation would not see the Promised Land. It took 40 years for the complaining generation to die off!

God delivered them out of captivity, promised them a land flowing with milk and honey, and they had the nerve to complain about food and water. Several times they wanted to turn back. When we ask "why me?" it tells God we are ungrateful. God never promised the journey to your dreams and goals would be all peaches and cream. Know that how you go through determines the length of time in the wilderness. If you survived what he delivered you from, why not trust Him to survive the wilderness and bring you to better?

Faith celebrates past victories regardless of present circumstances.

Yes You

In the words of T.D. Jakes, "Because you are anointed." You believed God. You trusted God. You stood on His word. You did not forget His promises. You did not allow your pain to consume you. You survived. You are running after God. You are living a life of holiness. If you are willing and obedient, you have no other choice! Once we decide to follow Jesus, purpose and destiny are unavoidable. Of course, you can choose to not follow Jesus.

However, if you weren't sick of your life, if you weren't tired of foolish decisions, if you weren't sick of living in mediocrity, if you weren't sick and tired of being sick and tired, and if you weren't curious of what true happiness was, then you wouldn't be a follower of Christ. Christianity has to be more than the heavenly promises of mansions, streets paved with gold, elimination of pain and suffering and the ability to see Jesus and our loved ones again. What about right now? What about the next 20, 40, 60 years that you will be on this side of heaven? There must be a reward for following God's commands?

Drifting along in life waiting for things to happen, going with the flow is not living. God is a good God to all. The sun shines on the just and the unjust. Shouldn't the pain and heartache you've experienced account for something? God promises beauty for ashes if we trust and follow him. My life, your life, human life is not in vain. If I can prevent someone from experiencing my pain and passing it on to the next generation, then I have lived a life worth living.

> *Faith does not have all the answers but faith trusts in the one who does.*

CHAPTER TWO
When God Stops Talking

Even in the silence, Faith knows to stand still until it recognizes God's voice. The word of God provides the water Faith needs to grow during the silence.

Does God really stop talking? Depends on who you ask and depends on your perception. No, God never stops talking, because even His silence has meaning. When Peter and the other disciples were in the boat with Jesus and the storms were raging and the boat was rocking, Jesus was asleep! His silence meant to trust Him. When Job lost everything and his friends and wife turned their backs on him, God's silence showed Job how strong he was in God and the measure of faith he had within.

Sometimes we can assume silence because God does not say what we want to hear. Though we may express that we are confused, crying for a word from the Lord, or declare our frustration in the wait, his instructions will not change.

In December 2014 I was laid off. The company I worked for lost their government contract and closed all Tennessee offices. I, and approximately 400 employees, found ourselves unemployed. We knew about 6 months in advance that the job was ending; the hunt was on for new employment. I took pride in praying for co-workers and watching God open doors for them. Even though I had been bitten by the entrepreneurial bug and was excited about my first book, "Stop Asking Why Are You Single," and its upcoming release, I did not think it was time to launch my own company and work for myself full-time. Despite clearly hearing God say He was going to give me a new business and the book would sell 10,000 copies; the thought still gave me pause. Somehow, I just knew God was not going to allow me to be unemployed and was going to give me another position in another company. But as I saw what God was doing for my co-workers, I couldn't help but feel left out. And yet, I also felt peace in knowing that whatever the outcome, I was going to be ok and God would take care of me.

By January reality set in. I was officially unemployed. I had worked my whole life since the age of 17. Working was all I knew. I have always taken care of myself. Now you mean to tell me I have to draw unemployment and get on food stamps? Clearly, there must be some mistake? Fifteen plus years in the workforce and my unemployment was only $275 per week, $247 after taxes. What's going on here? I know that's the max for Tennessee, but that will only cover the mortgage. What about food, utilities, car insurance, credit card bills, student loans, personal loans, etc.? I went into prayer. "I want you to write, I want to spend time with you, bask in my presence," says God. I began writing my 2nd book, "Saved, Single and Frustrated."

February came and I made it a whole month. People told me that it would take 6-8 weeks for my unemployment to kick in. I only waited 2 weeks. I filed for food stamps, and walked into that office praying that I did not run across any of my former clients. After presenting my unemployment benefit information, mortgage paperwork, and blue book value of my car, I only qualified for $32 a month in food stamps. Really?! How is that going to last a whole month? I called my mortgage company and found out they had an unemployment plan that allows homeowners to pay a portion of their mortgage for six months while looking for employment. I just had to wait for a decision. I called my personal loan company and discovered my loan officer signed me up for disability insurance that paid the loan in case of disability or unemployment. That was one bill I didn't have to worry about for up to six months. Still praying, God continued to encourage me to write and stay in His presence.

Hello March and Happy birthday to me! Surprisingly, that measly $247 per week is covering the bills. Not to mention I received two unexpected checks in the mail; one from a contracting instructor job I was doing but thought I wasn't going to get paid due to low attendance, and the other from my mortgage company! Apparently, I had extra funds in my escrow! I was scared to cash this one; I hadn't paid a mortgage in two months. That fear only lasted three days.

April rolled in and Thank you, Uncle Sam! Income taxes helped me get caught up on utilities and credit card bills. My mortgage company finally decided that I would pay $370 per month for six months or until I gained employment. What?! With what?! That's what they calculated I could afford based on my unemployment income. *Just breathe Indy. God will provide.* And provide He did! My friend was told about a seasonal job taking score at high school track meets. They paid $60 per game, but it was paid at the end of the season in a lump sum. The initial meeting was mid-March and she told me to go with her. Well, just by being there, I got the job too! Between March and April, we worked 24 games.

April showers bring May flowers. Thank you, Shelby County Schools. We received a lump sum of a little over $1300. Utilities, credit card bills, tithes and offerings quickly ate that up. Yes, I gave offerings to my church. I don't believe in coming into the Lord's house empty handed. Though I was unemployed I still gave an offering, even if only $10, every Sunday. Though I didn't have the income I wanted, God was still faithful and He was still providing. Nope, no job yet. "You are an employer producer, not an employee," God said to me, "Continue to write and stay in my presence."

By June I entered into six whole months of being unemployed. God took a little and made it stretch. "You have three weeks remaining," said the recording on the weekly unemployment certification call. *Breathe, Indy, Breathe! Lord what am I going to do?* Books not selling. My business is not making any money. I went on interviews but no one is calling. Why are you not listening to me? "Continue to write and stay in My presence," says God. "Saved, Single, and Frustrated" was completed end of June.

I received my last unemployment check on July 7. Ironically, "Saved, Single, and Frustrated" was released on Amazon and available for print that same day. Never mind that I completed my second book in six months, yet it took three years to finish the first; I could not enjoy the release of my second book as I was so worried about my finances and how I would pay the bills. My internet service was disconnected. Cable scheduled to be disconnected on August 11. Utility bill is now over $600. Car insurance is due. Vehicle registration is set to expire July 31.

Finding Faith

AND I got a ticket via US Postal Service for running a red light. A friend called and said she was moving to London and needed a place to stay while she worked her last three weeks on the job. She offered to pay me $100 per week. She moved in July 25 and stayed until August 14. Well, that paid for my car insurance and vehicle registration. When I found out the unemployment was ending I cried out to the Lord again in frustration. "The book is finished, now what?" "Continue to write," He said. "Write what?" I responded, "You have not given me the next book." Yes, I was trying to be sarcastic with God! "Ok, God what's next?" "Finding Faith," He replied. And here we are.

As I was studying the bible in my quiet time, God led me to the book of Numbers. Numbers continues the journey of the children of Israel out of captivity.

Whether it was two days, a month or a year that the cloud remained above the tabernacle, the children of Israel would remain encamped and not journey; but when it was taken up, they would journey. At the command of the Lord they remained encamped, and at the command of the Lord they journeyed; they kept the charge of the Lord at the command of the Lord by the hand of Moses.

—*Numbers 9: 22-23 (NKJV)*

God showed me that He was not silent. The cloud is above the tabernacle. He wanted me to remain encamped.

During encampment, spend time with Him, sup with Him, and bask in His presence. We are not to be concerned about the journey or when it will come. When the appointed time comes to move, you will know. Stop trying to journey when the Lord has said rest. Confusion is not of God. Confusion is a result of trying to move when God has commanded rest. While you are resting keep your eyes on God and watch His glory manifest. While I was worried about the bills, God had already paved a way.

Faith means acting on our beliefs. Faith and logic cannot co-exist. Intellect and reason clash with faith. Faith is rooted in the knowledge of God; however, the biggest myth is that God will always lead us to success. Though success may be the end goal, the journey may be difficult.

Hold on to God's Promises

Though it may appear that God is silent. His word says "be still and know that I am God." Regardless of what it looks like, we must learn to follow God's command and trust Him without question.

Faith does not always know where it is being led, but it loves, trusts, and knows He who is leading.

> Then she went and sat down across from him at a distance of a bow shot; for she said to herself "Let me not see the death of the boy." So she sat opposite him, and lifted her voice and wept. "And God heard the voice of the lad. Then the angel of God called to Hagar out of heaven, and said to her, "What ails you, Hagar? Fear not, for God has heard the voice of the lad where he is. Arise, lift up the lad and hold him with your hand, for I will make him a great nation."

—*Genesis 21: 16-15 (NKJV)*

Finding Faith

Until my storm, though I have read and heard Hagar's story plenty of times, I saw something different this time. God showed me three things:

1. Hagar separated from the promise to allow it to die. It appeared to be dying. At the first sign of trouble, the enemy immediately tells us that God is a liar, what He said can't be true. Our first thought is to give up or let go.

2. Hagar wept but God heard the voice of the lad. Replace the "lad" with whatever promise God has made you. In our frustration, during our pity party, the gift God gave us cries out to Him in fear of dying. If we give up or allow the gift to die, God cannot fulfill the promise. The promise is in the gift, not YOU. We have to stop making everything about us. God promised to make the gift great, the gift will make room for you, and the gift will bring you into the presence of great men.

3. God spoke to her. The first thing He said was, "Do Not Fear." Then He advised her to pick up the gift and reminded her of His promise. Do not allow fear to make you neglect God's gift. Do not allow fear of the unknown to stop you from being obedient. Lack comes through disobedience. As long as we are obedient to God's command, He is obligated to provide and take care of us. Your gift is required of you. God has returned for His talent. Are you doubling what you were given or did you bury it. Will God

Faith is holding on in the face of adversity. If adversity never comes, how do we know whether we can hold on? The beauty of it all is that God knows and has always known the amount of faith we possess.

declare you "good and faithful" or "wicked and lazy?" (Refer to the book of Matthew, parable of the talents).

The story of Job shows us that trials and tribulations are allowed by God. God's silence does not mean He is ignoring you or that you have done something wrong. Those trials could be to prove to you the measure of faith that is given you. At several points in my storm I questioned my faith. I even heard myself say I didn't have faith. But God showed me that the measure of faith, given to all, is not uncovered until the foundation is shaken.

Why Am I Here?

The myth of faith is that it is always unwavering. Abraham, the epitome of faith, wavered in his faith. He allowed Sarah to tell him to go into Hannah though God promised him a seed from his own body. He lied about Sarah being his wife when he journeyed into Egypt for fear of being killed because of her beauty. Yet God called Abraham a great man of faith. Wavering faith does not mean the same as lack of faith. Abraham still believed God.

Trials sometimes come so that God can show you who He is, who you are, and whose you are. There will come a time when you must know God for yourself. In the past you may have gotten by through the testimony of others. You heard God was a healer because he did it for Sister Jones. You heard God was a provider because He did it for Brother Smith. But now God must show you that He is the same God for you. He is no respecter of persons, what He does for one He does for all. During the trials, it is time to bond with the Lord, commune with Him. You are here for God to show you what He put in you and how He wants to use it in the Earth.

You have not done anything wrong. In fact, you have done it right. God is moving you to a new level. God is your everything. He is faithful. He will perform His word. Trust Him, know that He is working, and know that it is already done. Don't wait until you get what you want to praise Him. Praise Him now. Be grateful unto Him now. There is peace in your gratefulness. There is peace in His presence. Stay in God's presence. Fight for His presence. All and anything else are distractions. When we get out of God's presence, we become angry, frustrated, and confused. God has not changed His mind, He has not changed his plan, and you know his voice. When you cannot hear it is because you have drifted out of His presence. Do what He has commanded you to do. Focus on God.

Why are you here? Because you are anointed that's why!

Stick to the Plan

Whenever God gives us a promise, he always gives us a strategy to make it happen. When God told the children of Israel they would possess the land, he told them to march around the city a number of times and to sound the trumpet. After following His instructions, the walls of Jericho came tumbling down. Never mind that the army in that city outnumbered the children of Israel. God had already put fear in their hearts. When the walls came down the people feared their God and fled, leaving the city and its possessions behind. What if the children of Israel would have said, the instructions were silly and refused to follow? They probably would have been defeated by the larger army. Or perhaps they would have sat on the other side another 40 years.

Now the just shall live by faith; but if anyone throws back, My soul has no pleasure in him.

—Hebrew 10:38 (NKJV)

> *If you plan your own tomorrow, you eliminate the need for God to order your steps and therefore cannot be surprised when your miracle is a no show.*

There is no plan B with God. Why settle for less when God, the Alpha and Omega, He who knows the beginning and the end, has already promised you the best? Just because it is hard, just because the bank account is low, just because the bills are behind, just because no one is calling, just because you have no help, just because it appears the world is crumpling around you, does not mean you are to abort the plan.

Don't give up on your dream because the journey is not as you imagined. Don't give up on your dream because others don't understand or support you. Don't give up on your dream because of what today looks like. You may feel that you are not making progress but God is progressing you inside out. Your dream will be worth the sacrifice. You can't out strategize God, so stop trying. Stop trying to figure God out.

God had to show me that I was halting His

hand. His word says that He is our provider but we must allow Him to do so. How was I halting his hand you ask? By planning tomorrow and not living in the moment. If I had $20 in the bank, I would say I can't go anywhere today because I need to put gas in the car in case I need it for next week. I had allowed lack of money to stop me from enjoying life, used it as an excuse to not heed to God's instructions, and made it a source of my happiness. God does not want us to live in bondage. The word says we have not because we ask not. We cannot ask, and then figure our own way to get it. If you want God to be your provider, you must allow Him to provide. If you give your child $10 and immediately they go to the store and spend it all, but the next day they tell you they need lunch money; while you may question what they did with the $10 you gave them, you are still going to turn around and give them lunch money. This is the type of faith we must have in God. No we should not be foolish, taking the Lord's grace and favor for granted. However, we must take no thought for tomorrow and live for today.

CHAPTER THREE
If Only You Believed

Faith recognizes God's grace in the pain of the past. Faith understands that suffering does not change God's mind and believes that regardless of what is happening, victory is on the horizon.

Life happens . . .
It is what it is . . .
The struggle is real . . .
If it wasn't for bad luck, I wouldn't have any luck at all . . .
Why do bad things happen to good people . . . ?
The devil is busy . . .
Nobody understands me . . .
Life ain't easy, but it's fair . . .
What goes around comes around . . .
And my personal favorite:
You see my glory but you don't know my story . . .

The world has adapted and become accustomed to struggling. It's expected and considered the norm. Struggling is like a rite of passage to success. But how long will you stay there? What if I told you that the reason you struggle is because you allow yourself to be defined by your suffering? What if I told you that the reason you struggle is because you continue to allow your past to dictate your future? What if I told you that the reason you struggle is because of your pessimistic attitude? Would you change immediately?

Life does not just happen. It is not what it appears to be. The struggle is not real. Luck has nothing to do with it. Bad things don't just happen to good people. The devil is given too much credit. There is always someone who understands. Life is easy. The bible says the way of the transgressor is hard. You do reap what you sow, so what are you sowing? And the reason no one knows your story is because the enemy has you living in shame.

Hold Your Head Up

Your past is not a symbol of defeat. You do not have to live in shame and regret. In fact, you should be proud that you slept in the lions' den and came out untouched. Though the enemy threw you in the fiery furnace you came out with no burns nor did you suffer from smoke inhalation. In other words, you are alive, God did not allow it or them to kill you. What did you learn?

For in that He Himself has suffered being tempted, He is able to aid those who are tempted.

—Hebrews 2: 18 (NKJV)

What you suffered will help someone else who is also suffering. Someone is still in the lions' den. Someone is still in the fiery furnace. You know their story. You understand their pain. You know what they have been through. You know what it feels like to search for identity, to search for help, and to discover how to cope amongst people who had no clue. You know what it feels like to attempt to be visible among people who wanted to remain hidden. Identity shines the light of uniqueness amongst the darkness. In order to come out of poverty, out of darkness, out of pain, one has to be willing to be seen.

The world wants to tell you to suck it up, put your big girl panties on, and bear it. The enemy wants you to keep your mouth closed. Silence keeps you in bondage. Pray, encourage yourself, and call on the name of the Lord. As the old folks used to say, "A closed mouth don't get fed." You cannot receive help if you don't ask.

The world also wants to tell you that you should keep it to yourself. We all know that is a lie. There is a reason why underdog stories serve as motivation to others. Drama sells. Not because people enjoy seeing others hurt, but because people can relate to pain. Though our situations and experiences may be different, the pain, anguish, shame, regret, feelings of unworthiness, and wanting to give up is universal. Underdog stories give us hope, that if someone else made it, if someone else turned their sadness into success, if someone else turned their pain into prosperity, then we can to.

I remember I once asked the Lord, "Why is it that children living in poverty, in the ghetto or projects only see sports, music, or selling drugs as a way out of poverty?" He replied, "Because those are the only lifestyles filled with people who they can relate to." Rappers, football and basketball stars often tell their story of being raised by a single parent living in the projects. Some indicate how they had to sell drugs to provide for their siblings or to fund the beginning of their music careers. Our kids relate to that, they understand that struggle. On the contrary, how many times do we see doctors, lawyers, or other educated professionals tell the same story of being raised in the ghetto but going to school, continuing their education and now successful in their field? It is very rare. In order to change this, we as Christians, as believers have an obligation to those that come after us to tell our story, to give hope, that soon the rain will end if we don't give up.

Hold your head up! One day the storms will end. One day the sun will shine on you. One day the light will turn on and bring you out of the darkness. When one is drowning, the first thing they are told is to hold their head up. Why? So that they can prevent water from entering their body through the nose or mouth. Hold your head up! The more you look down, the more you notice the turmoil unfolding around you. Hold your head up! Look to the hills from whence cometh your help. Hold your head up! Always look for and expect help to come. As long as your head is up, you will see when help finally arrives.

Come from Among Them

One of the hardest things to do when you accept the call of God on your life is to separate from friends, loved ones, etc. You have to come from among them, because with them, your faults are interconnected.

Therefore "Come out from among them and be separate, says the Lord. Do not touch what is unclean, and I will receive you."

—*2 Corinthians 6:17*

Finding Faith

Birds of a feather flock together. I'm not like them, you say. But those on the outside looking in, group you all in the same category. If you are not like them, why are you with them? What do you have in common?

I remember in undergrad, as part of an assignment for my Social Work class, we had to go to an impoverished neighborhood, observe the people, and submit a written report on what we saw. As we approached the neighborhood, the first thing I noticed was the abundance of corner stores, liquor stores, and churches. Then I noticed the lack of grocery stores and entertainment venues. My classmates picked a spot and parked on the side of the street. We noticed a group of four teenage girls, dressed in short shorts or skirt and a tank top or halter top, walking down the street. As they walked, cars with men in them would pass by and whistle or yell out flirtatious words. "What's up Lil Mama?" "Hey, sexy chocolate," "Can I go with you?" etc. I noticed that while the girls would wave their hands signaling to leave them alone, they would be smiling and swaying their hips as they continued to walk. The girls would walk to the corner store and one or two would return with chips, soda, etc., in their hand. As we continued to observe them, we noticed that the same group of girls walked up and down that street for the entire hour that we sat there. As we watched,

Greatness sometimes, often times, has to walk alone. But Faith knows that walking alone is only for a short time.

several questions came to mind. Why did they continue to go back and forth to the store? Where were their parents? Why were they dressed in such skimpy attire? Wasn't there something better for them to do? Did we care if one or all of the girls was a straight A student and on the verge of a full scholarship to a university of her choice? Of all the assumptions we made of lack of home training, lack of role models, low self-worth, etc., excellent student was not one of them.

I said all that to say, who you associate with and the activities you take part in taint your image good or bad. Unfortunately, you are guilty by association. As a person who grew up in poverty and lived in the projects, I know that "fitting in" is sometimes not just about being liked but a matter of life and death. But in order to do better, to be better, you have to accept that you don't fit in and chose to come from among them.

God will always send someone to assist you or to walk with you. Once I decided I wanted more than fornication and having children out of wedlock, God sent me one friend who thought the way that I did. We became really close and pushed each other to finish high school and move out of the projects. Even now, as I walk towards my destiny, God has sent two or three church members who have become great friends to encourage and push me.

You may feel alone at first, but God just needs to get you away so that He can open your spiritual eyes. Once you have been enlightened, you will be receptive of what it takes to get to where He needs you to be. When you fully understand His plan and your role, then you will be able to go back and do much work there. First you have to recognize God's grace in the pains of your past. Then you have to allow Him to heal the wound.

Finding Faith

Once the wound is healed, allow Him to show you how to use it to bless others. But the prerequisite is that you must believe.

If Only You Believed

And we know that all things work together for good to those who love God, to those who are called according to His purpose. For whom He foreknew, He also predestined to be conformed to the image of His Son, that He might be firstborn among many brethren.

—Romans 8: 28-29 (NKJV)

The word says faith without works is dead, however, in order for all things to work for your good you must believe that it will. I began this chapter with the many clichés and phrases that people use when things are going wrong in their lives to show that what we get is a direct result of what we say. You speak what you believe. The word says that out of the abundance of the heart the mouth speaks. If you believed that all things worked for your good, you would say so. If you believed you were blessed, you would say so. If you believed that you were in the will of the Lord, you would act accordingly. If you believed that there was a purpose and a plan for your life, you would live accordingly.

Your defeatist attitude is a symbol of your unbelief.

Now He did not do many things mighty works there because of their unbelief.

—Matthew 13:58 (NKJV)

Believe that God can. Jesus died on the cross, so that we do not have to suffer for our sins. You are forgiven. Speak life.

Believe that God will. He came that we may have life and life more abundantly. It pleases Him to bless His children. Though it may tarry, the vision will speak and will not lie. God's promises are yeah and Amen.

Believe in the great I Am. You can do anything through Christ who strengthens you. Rely not on your strength, but His strength. Jesus had a moment of weakness on the cross when He yelled out, "Lord why has thou forsaken me?" But he came back to himself and said, "Nevertheless, thy will be done."

Believe in YOU. God chose you for a reason. Like I said before, somebody has to go first, somebody has to endure. Moses was afraid that his speech was not good enough. David thought he was merely a field hand. God knows what He is doing. He knows what He put in you. Trust his plan.

Believe in God's promises. God promises beauty for ashes and oil of joy for mourning. There is no waste in God. Your pain was not wasted. Your suffering was not wasted. Your time was not wasted. Your education is not a waste. Your money was not wasted. Your gifts and talents are not wasted. Stop allowing the enemy to tell you your life was a waste. God's

Belief is the work that activates your faith.

word will not return to Him void. You shall see His glory.

Believe that God will restore. The bible says that whatever the thief stole he must repay seven-fold. Job got double for his trouble. Your enemies will become your footstool. When God does it, all will know it was Him!

Believe that God will provide. In whatever state you are in believe that God is there with you and will supply all your needs. His word promised He would be our provider, but we must let Him. The time has come for you to be solely dependent on God. It is the only way you will make it to the Promised Land. It is the only way that you will learn to trust Him.

Believe that God is faithful. Don't allow the enemy to magnify your mistakes. This journey is one of faith, not perfection.

David was a man after God's own heart not because he did everything right, we know he had many shortcomings, but because he accepted correction and was quick to repent and get back in line.

Faith knows there is no failure in Christ. God's word will never lead you where His grace cannot protect you.

Recognize What is Detrimental to Your Belief

We all know the story of the children of Israel's journey out of bondage. In Numbers 14, the anger of the Lord grew so, that He swore that they would not see the Promised Land. What they did is a testament to understanding how we allow unbelief to cause us to miss the blessings of the Lord.

The first sign of unbelief is complaining. The Lord had brought the children out of captivity and it seems like they complained the whole journey. Just reading the story I found myself mad. But are we, this generation, any different? God does and has done so much for us, yet when a new, seemingly more difficult, problem arises, we immediately start complaining, comparing our life to others and questioning why God allowed such a bad thing to happen.

I hated going to work at FedEx. Not because it was a difficult job or because I disliked my managers and co-workers but because I knew I wanted to be doing something better. I always wanted to help people find a better quality of life. I wanted to give back to my community. I appreciated my job. It paid the bills and funded my college education, I formed great relationships and learned a lot about business and professionalism. But I wanted more. I had been looking for new employment for years but nothing seemed to work out or would pay me comparable to what I was making. During my second Master's degree I discovered I wanted to help impoverished people find jobs, housing, etc., so I researched companies who had the

You are not required to do everything right, but you are required to have faith. Faith gives you a heart of gratitude and repentance.

same mission. I found three and looked weekly on their websites for job openings, applying for any and every opening I thought I was qualified for. Finally, I got an interview with a company who helps welfare recipients find employment and educational opportunities to get out of poverty. Sounds perfect doesn't it? It was, until I got the job offer. The pay was considerably less annually than what I was making at FedEx. I was heartbroken. I went into prayer and clearly heard the Lord say, "I am your provider, I will provide, trust me." So I took the job.

A few months into the job, I started to feel the absence of that money I wasn't getting. I began to complain and even pondered getting a second job. But as months went on I saw that though I was making less, I still didn't miss a beat. The bills were paid. I still shopped as I wanted. I still traveled as I wanted. I learned that God is faithful even when we doubt Him.

The second sign of unbelief is going back to the place of deliverance. Many times, on the journey the children of Israel indicated it would have been better for them to stay in Egypt. How could captivity be better than freedom? This is what God is saying to us today. How can bondage be better than freedom? When the above job I spoke about ended, the first question I posed to God was, "Why did you take me from FedEx to allow me to be unemployed? At least there I had job security." But how soon did I forget how miserable and unappreciated I felt there. How soon I forgot that I asked the Lord for a job with meaning and the ability to make a difference in the lives of others. How soon I forgot the joy I felt as I formed relationships with my new clients and facilitated change in their lives. How soon I forgot the sense of accomplishment I felt when my clients brought me cards and flowers to thank me for helping them obtain the resources they needed. How soon I forgot how thankful I was when I first got the new job. How quickly I allowed the cares of the world to make me forget that it wasn't about me but about the people. God does not deliver His people to return them to bondage. God does not bless His people to later take it back. I had to learn to trust His plan, even when mid-way through times got tougher.

Another sign of unbelief is worry. Worry and faith cannot coexist. You can either worry about it or pray about it. You can't do both, as one cancels out the other. I thought when I left FedEx I had a pay cut. But heck I was making it. Then when the job ended I went to one-third of my salary through unemployment. When I look back on the many nights I spent unable to sleep, head hurting, tears burning my pillow thinking about how I was going to pay this and that, I know now it was all for nothing. God already knows what the end will be. God already knows how He will provide. I lost sleep for nothing. At times I felt like I added to my own misery by refusing to trust God. By refusing to believe that He was still in control. Eight months later I have not gone without anything. God promised in His word that His seed would not beg for bread. All God requires is faith.

The enemy tried to tell me that I did not know God's voice or that I wasn't hearing Him

Faith does not yearn for the past even if it is falling forward.

Finding Faith

correctly. Many days and nights I prayed and fasted for direction. I would constantly hear God say, "I want you to write, stay in my presence, just write." Clearly that was not all He wanted me to do. I needed a job! But guess what, no one was calling! I sent out three to five resumes a week. Called them after two weeks to check if the position was open. The receptionist would say someone would get back to me and then miraculously I would get an email a week later stating the position had been filled. I even took my degrees off my resume in hopes of getting a basic customer service position or work at a temp agency. Guess what? Nobody called me back. I cried out to the Lord. His response was, "I'm giving you this time to rest, stay in my presence and write." Though I felt like writing couldn't be all He wanted me to do, writing was all I knew to do. Writing kept me in perfect peace, I felt His presence, and I heard His voice. I learned that just because times get tough, in our eyes, God does not change His mind.

Another sign of unbelief is fear. How is it that we can request and want something from the Lord, yet when it is presented before us we become afraid because it was not packaged the way we expected? The children of Israel begged for freedom, but did not know it would lead them to wandering in the wilderness not having a place to lay their head. I had always dreamed

True faith is confidence that God will. Not that He can, but that He will.

of working for myself. After the publication of my first book I often dreamed about the life of a writer, traveling and speaking, meeting new people, etc. But when faced with it, I allowed the fear of inconsistent income to bombard my thoughts and distract me from God's plan. How could I proclaim to be a writer, yet when God told me to write, I refused? In my mind, I was a part-time writer and full-time Career Counselor. I was trying to build my Career Counseling business and writing on my book once or twice a week. In my mind, the book was not selling as fast as I thought it should, so I took that to mean perhaps my writing was just a hobby or side hustle. But God showed me that He called me to write.

Faith understands that God's purpose and plan do not take a backseat to your own personal plan.

Even if what we want and what God has in store are one in the same, the journey will be totally different and unexpected. Why? Because God wants complete control. If we are able to do it on our own, why would we need God? Remember, in the end, God gets the glory not you.

Believe in the impossible. Believe that though you cannot see or understand His plan, that He does have a plan and that plan is to give you hope and an expected end. Faith is like being stuck in a corner of a burning building. The fireman enters the building. He is calling your name. Though you hear him, you cannot move because debris

Finding Faith

from the building is falling and crumbling all around you. You yell out, "I'm up here." Just when you think you are going to pass out and die, the fireman is standing in front of you. He picks you up and as he holds you in his arms you wrap your arms tightly around his neck. He whispers in your ear, "Everything is going to be all right, I got you now." You muzzle up a smile and as he turns headed back toward safety, the debris is still falling and the fire is getting hotter and hotter. With each fall of debris, you scream and hold on tighter. As your voice appears to be getting louder you notice He is not saying anything, he just keeps walking. In the distance you see a light, but behind you, you still see debris falling and fire blazing. "Almost there," he whispers. His words cause an abrupt stop to the screams, but you are still crying. Finally, after several steps, you feel the breeze of fresh air on your neck. You turn and see that you have made it outside, he places your feet on solid ground. As you stand, you wipe your eyes, turn and say, "Thank you." He smiles and says, "Just doing my job, ma'am." Jesus wants you to know He is just doing His job. He came in this world to give you life and regardless of how bad it gets, how hard it seems, He will always be there to carry you through. Just trust and believe that help is on the way. He hears your cry. Hold on to him, and He will lead you to safety.

CHAPTER FOUR

Fear of the Unknown

Faith relinquishes control and allows God to guide it into uncharted territory because it knows that everything it seeks is on the other side of its comfort zone.

Taking my daily scroll down my timeline on Facebook, I came across a question posed by a friend. He asked, "Would you quit your job without already having secured another position?" Of the 55 comments received on this post, 90% said, "No," citing reasons regarding the current economy, difficulty in finding employment, wisdom from parents, belief that the employed are more employable, or consideration for basic necessities and support to other family members. Of the 10%, including myself, who said, "Yes," we answered with the same or similar response, "Sometimes you have to step out on faith."

No sooner than I hit enter to post my response, I heard the Holy Spirit ask, "Would you have responded the same way one or two years ago?" "Nope," I answered. "Did you make the choice or did I make it for you?" Reluctantly I answered, "You made it for me." I too believed that you didn't quit a job before finding another one. I too believed that your personal responsibilities were more important than your wants or desires. I too believed that it was better to stay where you were and bear the unhappiness, until something better came along.

Jesus said to him, "Thomas, because you have seen Me, you have believed. Blessed are those who have not seen and yet have believed.

—John 20:29 (NKJV)

I know the above scripture is pertaining to belief in Jesus as the Son of God and dying on the cross for our sins, but the Holy Spirit brought it to my remembrance at that moment as well. God reminded me that before our faith is tested, before we develop a relationship with Him, we cannot comprehend the type of blind faith necessary to take the leap into the unknown.

Most of us, many of us have to be pushed into the deep. Why? The fear of the unknown paralyzes us, and prevents us from utilizing the full power of He that is within us.

At some point, in order to enter into the promises of God, we will have to relinquish control and allow God to guide us into uncharted territory. At some point we will all be faced with this question: "Do you want the promise or do you want what's familiar?"

Totally Dependent on Him

If you could do it on your own, why do you need God? If you could get there by your own abilities and strength, why do you seek God? Before you can enter the Promised Land,

Finding Faith

you must learn to rely totally on God, heed His instructions, and trust His will.

Though He was a Son, yet He learned obedience by the things which He suffered. And having been perfected, He became the author of eternal salvation to all who obey Him

—Hebrews 5: 8-9 (NKJV)

In our sufferings, though hard as it may seem, God is drawing us to Him. It is imperative that we do not revert back or allow distractions to cause us to doubt the hand of God. In the end we will be stronger and wiser for His use. When you get to the point where you realize there is nowhere else to turn to, nothing else you can do, or nobody who can help you BUT God, you are exactly where God wants you to be.

Unemployment is scary. Facing the inability to care for oneself and his/her family is enough to cause tremble in anyone. With no money in the bank, no income or money expected, no new employment awaiting me, I have an unexplainable peace. All I hear the Lord saying is, "Trust Me." I remember crying out to God, "I don't know what to do." I clearly heard, "This time I want you to do nothing, be still and watch my glory manifest." Don't get me wrong, like I said before, unemployment is scary. When the

Faith is perfected through suffering. Suffering teaches obedience.

bills are due I have to remind myself that God is faithful. When depression and low self-esteem creep up, I have to tell myself God is able.

When I tell you that God will put you in a place where you have no choice but to trust Him, that's exactly what I mean. I did not ask to be unemployed. I did not quit my job by choice. I did not even think or foresee that my unemployment would last this long. But I do know God is faithful. He has taken care of me before so I know He will take care of me now. I remember in 2006, when I left an adulterous relationship. I obtained a second job to make ends meet. I was too tired to enjoy the fruits of my labor and too afraid to quit for fear of not being able to take care of the bills. God allowed me to get fired. What I thought was unmanageable with income from one job turned out to be more than enough. I also remember in 2009 when I foolishly decided to stop paying my mortgage because I wanted a modification and the bank/lender would not intervene unless I was behind, I watched God remedy a situation in spite of my own mistakes. I went eight months without paying a mortgage, and God turned that thing around in my favor. God honored His covenant.

I stand today in the face of adversity, with a memory of what God has done before and faith that He can do even greater works. I stand today with a confidence that God is not a liar. I stand

In the face of adversity, faith rests in the victories of yesterday.

Finding Faith

today in anticipation of a marvelous testimony that is to follow. This is what God calls us to do. In the face of trials and tribulations, He wants us to remember that He is not punishing us rather He is drawing us to Him. He is teaching us to trust and rely on Him. He is showing us the measure of faith He instilled in us at creation. Before this journey, I thought I had no patience, I thought I lacked faith. I have learned that faith is not something WE can see. The seed is planted by God. Our trials are the rain that is required to make the seed grow. And it is God who gets the increase.

When God brings you out, when God opens the door, you and even your enemies will know that it was nobody but God who did it.

Dive into the Deep

The story of Peter walking on the water is one of my favorite stories. It is a reminder that if we keep our eyes on Jesus we will not drown. It is a reminder that at the same time that we are walking toward Jesus, He is walking towards us. It is a reminder that taking our eyes off Jesus, even for a second, is a matter of life and death. It is a reminder that regardless of the outcome, regardless of what lies ahead, you must first get out the boat!

> *Faith is the ability to trust God enough to get out of your comfort zone. Staying there is always an option and is often safer. But miracles don't happen in the safety area.*

When Jesus turned water into wine, there were hundreds of guests and a pushy mother awaiting Him. When Peter walked on water, the deep ocean that was the final resting place of many was beneath him. When Jesus fed the multitude, there were over 5000 men, women, and children, one fish, two loaves of bread, and land and water to the left and right of them. Would faith had been needed if there was a liquor store next to the wedding chapel or more wine in the cellar? Would faith had been needed if the boat was only 3 feet away from the shore? Would faith had been needed if Jesus delivered his sermon next to a supermarket? Of course not, faith manifests when only God can intervene. Faith is needed when only God can provide the answer.

> *Faith is not just a way through which we obtain God's promise. It is a way of life. All that are of the faith did not receive the promise.*

Worry is the ride or die chick of fear. Where there is fear, there is worry. We are unable to trust God to launch into the deep, to go into the unknown, because of worrying. We worry about finances, failure, success, approval of others, hatred or envy from others, whether we are good enough, our own abilities, past mistakes, losing friends, alienating loved ones, being alone, being on the forefront, outer appearance, etc. The list is never ending. To dive into the deep, one has to do so in spite of fear, in spite of worry, and because of God. Some of us, if we knew what would happen, still would come up with another excuse, another thing to fear, another thing to worry about.

Now faith is the substance of things hoped for, the evidence of things not seen. For by it the elders obtained a good testimony.

—*Hebrews 11: 1-2 (NKJV)*

Abraham did not live to see all his descendants. Abel was killed because of his faith. Faith is "going on" in holiness knowing that God is able and will perform the promise. Faith does not know when the promise will come, but knows that God is a rewarder of those who diligently seek Him. Faith is seeking God in everything, through everything, because He is faithful and just.

Faith never dies. Your testimony lives on after you.

We are still reminded of the blood of Abel crying out from the ground. We are still reminded of the faithfulness of Abraham by whom we receive the inheritance. We are reminded of Paul, John the Baptist, etc., who were imprisoned, beaten, chained, stoned, beheaded, afflicted, tormented, etc., for the pure love and faithfulness of God. Someone is always watching. Someone always listening. Someone is always recording. Someone will continue the story. Someone will pick up the torch and resume the race.

Keep the faith not just for you, not just for

materialistic gain or riches. Keep the faith to inspire others to do the same. Faith is a reminder of things to come and invokes joy in knowing that every day is a day closer to the ultimate prize of a relationship with Jesus.

Dive into the deep knowing that regardless of the outcome, God is with you. If you trust Him, you too will walk on water. You are not supposed to know how to swim. It is the possibility of failure that sends a request for the supernatural powers of God. Yes, failure is always a possibility, but so is success. One thing for sure, if you stay in the boat, if you stay in your comfort zone, you will never know what could have been.

How do you know God is pushing you out of your comfort zone? When you begin to detest mediocrity. When you have a gut feeling that there is more out there for you to do. When you know there is something better awaiting you. When you are sick and tired of being sick and tired. When the option of failing is more appealing than allowing things to stay the same. When you realize you have nothing to lose. When you are tired of life passing you by. When you are tired of living vicariously through others. When you realize that good things don't just happen. When you realize that where there is no risk, there is no reward.

Fear is normal. Fear is going to come knocking whether you invite him or not. But when you decide to look fear right in the face and do it anyway. Heart pounding, palms sweating, no goggles, no snorkels, no fins, no air tank, etc., dive right on in, knowing that sink or swim you still win. You will realize that once you have the courage to dive in, not giving up is easier.

Finding Faith

Don't Give Up

And so after he had patiently endured, he obtained the promise.

—Hebrews 6:15 (NKJV)

What does it really mean to endure? I used to think of endure as a synonym for patience. But actually, endure means "to carry on through, despite hardships; undergo or suffer; to suffer patiently without yielding." In other words, endurance involves holding on, during and in spite of suffering. Faith does not feel good.

Nobody wants to suffer. Which is probably why, in telling us the promise, God leaves that part out. Our self-preserving selves would stop before we even got started.

You must learn to keep going. The enemy comes to stop you, to prolong, to hinder, and to offend. No matter what, don't give up. Don't stop praying. Don't stop communing with God. Don't stop seeking His presence. The more you seek His presence, the more He will draw you in. Don't stop believing that all things are possible. God cannot lie. His word is not a lie. Remember it is only a test. Remember it is only temporary.

Don't allow your thoughts to distance you from God. Fight for His presence. Sometimes waiting for the storm to pass is the hardest and

> *Faith does not always take us through Mr. Roger's neighborhood on the way to the promise.*

scariest thing to do. The devil is telling you, "You are going to die," but that small still voice is telling you, "just a little while longer." Remember, God is the peace in the eye of the storm. Stay focused. Remember the word. You have come too far to turn back. Going back would be more detrimental than moving forward.

As a writer, during my storms, the first thing I tend to do is stop writing. My mind is bogged down from fretting. I can't seem to hear from God. My stomach is in knots from stressing. Headaches are more frequent. I want to do nothing but sleep, eat and watch television. After about two or three weeks of foolishness, I hear the Holy Spirit say, "you're drifting, come back." I have to literally fight back. I start reading the word. Sometimes it takes me reading the same chapter in two or three versions to get an understanding. But I read anyway. I watch sermons on YouTube. I watch Joyce Myers (my favorite author and minister) on television. But the one thing that surely brings me back is God will send someone else that brings a word to my remembrance. He will send a friend or teenager that needs counseling or a word of encouragement, and the same words they need will surely apply to me. It is in those times that I am reminded that God will not allow His children to drift too far out of His presence. If we don't harden our hearts.

The enemy uses trials to tell us that we are being punished, have done something wrong, or are not worthy of what God promised. I find that we cannot fight that battle alone. Honesty in the face of God is the answer. Sometimes during warfare, the most needed thing to do is the most difficult. Yes, I am talking about prayer. There will come a time when the suffering feels unbearable and giving up is simpler. Just remember that the simplest prayers pack the most impact. Just the other day, all I could muster up was, "Jesus help me!" and the tears began to flow. I told God how I was feeling and that I knew it was not of Him because the word says . . . blah blah blah. Afterwards I felt relieved and miraculously the voices in my head stopped and the headache was gone. The word silences the enemy.

Fight not to give up. Fight for His presence. The word says, "come to me all who are heavy laden and I will give you rest." A fancy prayer filled with thee, thus, thou, etc., is not necessary, all God requires is one that is from the heart. Call a friend or prayer warrior and ask them to pray with you. Find a prayer online to read when you don't know what to say. Pray for others. I believe it is human nature to see the issues of others better than we can see our own. Plus, it is easier to do things for others than we can do for ourselves. This is also therapeutic in that God says what you do for others, He will make happen for you. So, while you are praying for someone else, someone is praying for you.

Remember trials come to make you stronger. God has to show you what is in you. They invoke spiritual growth. You can't stay on milk all your life, you must move on to solid foods. Trials also reveal the character of God. With each lesson you learn who God is to you and for you. With each trial you are strengthened for the next. The

The journey of faith does not promise to be easy but it does produce a great reward to those who refuse to give up.

test of faith is like taking a computer-generated test of knowledge. With each correct answer, the next question is harder. Those who have great faith, did not obtain it overnight. Trials and tribulations made them tougher. God has to make you unstoppable. No matter what comes your way, it will not stop the plan of God in your life. No matter what comes your way it cannot stop you from pursuing and fulfilling your purpose.

Don't give up! Friends, family, co-workers, future generations, etc., are depending on you. Someone is observing you. You must show them that following God is the best and only option. Don't give up! God promised your latter days will be greater. To whom much is given, much is required. Someone once told me that "our valley experience is an indication of our mountain top success." In other words, great prosecutions proceed great success. Don't allow the enemy to throw you off course. Abundant life is available to all, but it is the road less traveled, because of fear of the unknown and the inability to come out of one's comfort zone.

CHAPTER FIVE

Are you Ready for What You Asked for?

Faith is finding contentment in every situation and being prepared when the promise comes not when you expect it.

Are you ready for what you asked for? If presented with your wildest dream right now, would you embrace it? If it came wrapped in a package you did not expect, would you recognize it?

Then Caleb quieted the people before Moses and said, "Let us go up once and take possession, for we are well able to overcome it." But the men who had gone with him said, "We are not able to go up against the people, for they are stronger than we." And they gave the children of Israel a bad report of the land which they had spied out, saying, "The land through which we have gone as spies is a land that devours its inhabitants, and all the people who we saw in it are men of great stature. There we saw giants (the descendants of Anak come from the giants); and we were like grasshoppers in our own sight, and so we were in their sight."

—Numbers 13: 30-33

Indiana Tuggle

This is a very pivotal point in the journey of the children of Israel. I'm not sure how many days out of captivity and into the journey they were, but it is here that God sent them to spy out the land. God had already told them that He was going to give the land to them, they were just given a peek into the promise. What is interesting is that it is these 3 verses that ignited the anger of the Lord and after which He declared this generation would not see the Promised Land. Caleb was the one who believed they could conquer the land. It never said that Caleb did not see the giants! Regardless of what he saw, it was irrelevant, he believed God, and he had faith.

Favor opens the door, but faith must walk through it.

Faith is looking in the face of the impossible, looking in the face of trouble, looking in the face of fear and literally looking in the face of giants and declaring thus said the Lord. There will come a time when God will send you to spy out the land. You are well able to conquer it, however what you receive is dependent upon what you see and how you see yourself.

I remember before my job ended and after the release of my first book, I often fanaticized about the life of a writer. Traveling city to city, state to state and eventually country to country having book signings, book events, etc. Meeting different people and enjoying life with no boundaries. Having the ability to write wherever and whenever the inspiration hit. Becoming a

Finding Faith

best-selling author, television and radio interviews, speaking before large crowds, etc., I prayed to one day become a full-time author. Then when the job ended, I allowed the worries and cares of finances and making ends meet to cloud my vision and halt my dreams. Often times I would hear the Lord say, "I gave you this time to write." But writing was the last thing I wanted to do. Honestly, I couldn't write, my mind was so bogged down that I couldn't hear anything beyond my worries.

A few weeks ago, embarking on month nine of unemployment, I heard the Lord say, "I gave you what you asked for, you are as great as you say you are." I literally had to take a step back. Was I enjoying the life of a writer? Or was I complaining because it did not come in the package I expected? At first, I was having a ball. I got up every morning, prayed, went to the gym, came home cooked breakfast, had a cup of coffee and spent hours in the presence of the Lord writing. Then the praying ceased. I didn't feel like going to the gym. And writing began to feel more like a task than a privilege. Why? I began to doubt my abilities as a writer. Books weren't selling. I didn't know how to market. No speaking engagements. No events. No money to purchase books or even a booth at events. I allowed the cares of the world to taint my view. I needed a job and in my mind nothing else mattered. Writing books was not paying the bills. I was frustrated, I was angry, and I was confused. Nothing seemed to work. I kept hitting brick walls. What was I doing wrong? Was I extending my wilderness time? Was I seeing giants in my Promised Land? Was I viewing myself as a grasshopper?

Examine Yourself, Check Your MMA's

Time in the wilderness does not always mean that you have done or are doing something wrong. However, it is very important that we constantly examine ourselves to ensure we are going through on the correct path and not circling the same mountain. MMA's are your mind, mood, and attitudes.

Mind—Are your thoughts in line with the word of God? The bible tells us that so a man thinketh so he is. We must always be mindful of the promises of God and think on things that are of a good rapport. Don't allow the enemy to cloud your mind with thoughts of inadequacy (what you can't do), fear (afraid of the outcome), loneliness (cheering section is empty), or envy (others have it better than you). Remember that if God said it, you are able to do it. Remember fear is not of God and failure is not an option as long as God is in control. Remember that you are never alone, God is always with you, and in His word, He promised to never leave nor forsake you. Remember that envy is one of the Ten Commandments. Don't be envious of others, don't grow weary in well doing, for in due season you shall reap if you faint not.

Finding Faith

Mood—Do you allow your present circumstances to affect your mood and actions? Remember to just walk by faith and not by sight. Learn to encourage yourself. Learn to be happy and content regardless. Learn to enjoy whatever stage in the journey God has you in. Learn to speak life and joy to your situation regardless. Learn to hold your head up when questioned by others.

Attitude—Do you allow your present circumstances to affect your attitude? We should always represent an attitude of gratitude. Be thankful to the Lord always. Learn to praise Him in advance. Learn to thank Him in advance. As the old folks say, learn to fake it until you make it.

The MMA check is not always pleasant. Because I did not have the money or financial security I felt came along with the life of a writer, I doubted my ability as a writer. Because I did not have a book deal or the books were not selling, I doubted my ability as a writer. Because I kept hitting brick walls in my efforts to promote my books or obtain speaking engagements, I doubted myself as a writer. You see the pattern here? The enemy comes to steal, kill, and destroy (steal your dreams, kill your hope and destroy your future). He does so by telling you, you are not what God says you are. Man cannot validate you. Man cannot exalt you. Man cannot deny what God has already confirmed. We have to stop looking for and expecting worldly confirmations for God's anointing and callings on our life. A thousand no's cannot cancel out one yes from God.

God always gives a strategy for what He has called us to do. Unfortunately, the strategy will be given one step at a time. Time is in God's hand. He determines the appropriate time to proceed to the next step. You need this time, this place, so that

God can show you who you are: your strength, your abilities, and His power in you. Remember you are as great as you say you are. Remember God is with you, and because He is with you, you are able to do it.

Never Give Up

Fight not to give up. There will come a time when the wilderness, the pain, the suffering will become seemingly unbearable, and you will be tempted to give in.

Faith understands that purpose is greater than self-preservation.

Lest there be any fornicator or profane person like Esau, who for one morsel of food sold his birthright. For you know that afterward, when he wanted to inherit the blessing he was rejected, for he found no place for repentance though he sought it diligently with tears.

—Hebrews 12: 16-17

Don't sell your birthright for immediate gratification. What you are tempted with, may feed you now, but what God has for you, you will never hunger again. Trust God's plan. We are often tempted to intervene. To try to make things happen for ourselves. Only to regret it later. Yes, what God has for you is for you, but you can mess it up . . . if you give up.

You are responsible and held accountable for

what God tells you and instructs you to do. Don't settle for less because you want to satisfy your flesh now. Regardless of what it looks like, regardless of what other people say, you must hold on to the voice and promises of God. Unemployment is difficult. What's more difficult are the many friends, family, loved ones, etc., constantly telling you, "you need a job!" The statement may be true, but in essence, what I hear is, "you need to let go of your pride and take any job, you got bills to pay." And that I cannot do. Many call it stubborn but I call it faith. God promised me a career, not just a job. I will not settle. I will not give up my birthright, I will not walk away from the promises of God, to pay the bills.

God has given you a vision. Where there is no vision the people perish. Why? Because they are tossed to and fro with no direction. People with no vision, chase money. We all know that money can come and go with the blink of an eye. But purpose can never be taken. Also, where there is no sacrifice, there is no reward.

You must not give up. Like with Esau, it may not come around again. Though the wilderness may seem tough and unbearable, God is teaching you to fish. He is teaching you to be totally dependent on Him. Pain draws us closer to God. When we hurt or are hurting we are more willing to fall to our knees and go to God in prayer. Though you are hurting, you are exactly where God wants you to be. Your heart is open, your mind is clear, you are more receptive of His instructions. Though the enemy wants you to feel defeated, or that you have nowhere else to turn, God is requesting that you hand it over to Him. He does not need your help anyway.

You must not give up. Remember this is only a test. Oh,

the people you will bless with your testimony. Remember this time, this moment and this pain, is bigger than you. It's about the kingdom. Don't allow the enemy to cause you to be fearful, to be full of worry or to disturb your peace. Fight past your feelings. You must trust God. Your life, your dreams and future generations, are depending on you. But you must not give up.

Count It All Joy

My brethren, count it all joy when you fall into various trials, knowing that the testing of your faith produces patience. But let patience have its perfect work, that you may be perfect and complete, lacking nothing.

—James 1:2-4

It is the word that transforms, that perfects, that slays the enemy, and that causes Heaven to rise in our defense.

When we are going through, the last thing we want to hear is "count it all joy." It doesn't feel good and it is not a joyous occasion. But it's your attitude while going through that depletes your joy. We cannot allow the trials to steal our joy. Joy cannot be predicated on earthly materials or pleasure. The joy of the Lord is your strength. Your strength is found in the word.

When we are going through various trials, the first thing the enemy convinces us to do is to stop praying and reading the word. Why? We assume we need to do something to change things. We assume that praying and reading will not help. The problem with this is, we are trying to fight our battles in our own strength. But our situation cannot be changed by our own might, we cannot do it alone. Allow God, His word, to give you strength. We must understand that we cannot put down our weapons, (the word) when in battle.

When we put down the word, we remove ourselves from God's protection. We invite the enemy of frustration, confusion, fear, pride, anger, depression, etc., to come in and raise havoc. It is really hard to be frustrated, confused, fearful, etc., in God's presence! When these feelings arise, and/or when you begin to doubt, ask yourself when was the last time you prayed or read the word?

When in the wilderness, we must be mindful that we are in warfare at all times. We must stay alert. We must stay in His presence. An idle mind is the devil's playground. I never knew or understood the depth of that cliché until now. When soldiers are at war, someone is on guard at all times. They rotate those who will stand guard and those who will sleep throughout the night.

When in the wilderness we don't have time for frivolous or mindless activities. God reminded me that too much time on social media, watching TV, etc., was not only unproductive but it causes us to lose focus. Our guards are down. Our minds are distracted. Therefore, when the enemy attacks we are unprepared.

When in the wilderness, we must safeguard our eyes and ears. We must be conscious of what we see, watch, and hear. Is what we watch or listen to promoting the word of God and its kingdom? The world tells us to beware of becoming a pseudo-saint or becoming so holy that we are no earthly good. Funny how people can say you are too holy or call you a Jesus freak, but nobody tells you when you are partying *too* much, having sex *too* much, cursing *too* much etc. But anyway, if you allow too much trash to come in, then when the enemy appears you will not be able to fight him off. If it's not nurturing your spirit, empowering your thoughts and actions, or encouraging your heart, then it needs to be limited.

"Count it all joy" does not mean that you are to be happy that you are hurting. But rather it means, that you find pleasure in knowing that your future must be pretty awesome, that the devil is trying to stop you from reaching it. It means that you are in the will of God, because the devil has no beef with those already on His team. It means that God chose you, to be a light on the hill for those in darkness. It means that you are to rejoice because it is only temporary and victory is on the way. It means that God is preparing you for what is to come, so that when it comes you will be able to handle it.

"Count it all joy" means that you realize that you will come out perfect, complete, and lacking nothing on the other side. I have learned that "lacking nothing" is not an indication or promise that you will have everything you want when you want it. It means that you have everything you need in God. There is no lack in God. How can

Faith produces the ability to wait on God. The inability to wait causes lack.

Finding Faith

you have lack, following a God who has everything?

I have learned that lack is assumed in impatience. Constantly trying to figure God out causes lack. Faith is not concerned with the when and the how. Faith just trusts. I had to learn to stop the, "I need this and that by this date," kind of prayers. God does not work on our timetables. My problem was I wanted things to be done ahead of time, to ease my anxiety. But God explained to me that I needed to learn how to rest in knowing that He will supply all my needs. When we give God deadlines we set ourselves up for failure. It doesn't take God long to do anything. What seems like days to us is but a few hours to Him.

In September 2015, I was worried about my electricity being cut off. I received a cut off notice in the mail. The bill was $635 and I needed to pay $240 in two weeks to keep it on. I did what I knew to do. I went to the Community Services Agency (CSA) to ask for assistance for the second time. Though they did not help the first time, I was praying that this time would be different. However, they have 90 days to decide and tell you to continue making payments. *I'm unemployed, how can I continue making payments?* I also completed an online application for MIFA for assistance as well. No response. One week passed. I called and got an extension, which gave me an additional week to get the funds. Well, my brother and my mother gave me $100 each and I asked a friend for the other $40. Meanwhile, I am crying and praying, telling God, "You promised to take care of me."

The day after Labor Day I went to the utility office to make my payment, mind you that I received an updated bill in the mail and with current charges the bill is now $860. Thankful that I got the $240 needed to keep it on, I went through the drive through to make my payment. "You're paying $240," said the clerk. "Yes Ma'am," I responded. "Ok, thank you Ms. Tuggle, have a great day," she said. When she gave me the receipt back for my payment, I looked at the balance and noticed it said my balance is $179. HUH!? So, who paid over $400 on my bill? I had already driven off, so I couldn't ask her. I went online to see if the payment had posted, nope online is still showing $860. So, I waited a few days and went online again. Three days later it shows my payment of $240 and a balance of $620. Now I'm confused, so I called the billing hotline. Put in my address, phone number, etc., and the automated service stated my balance is $179. It is now a week later and I still do not know which agency paid my bill but I am grateful.

I said all that to say, "count it all joy" in knowing that when you are in God's will and taking care of His business, He will handle your business. The word says His seed will not beg for bread. That includes begging Him.

Show Me Your Works

Thus also faith by itself, if it does not have works, is dead.
—James 2:17

Your actions must reflect what you believe. Waiting is an action. Patience is an action. Worry and depression are also actions, but they show lack of faith. A few months ago, I quoted that scripture, "Faith without works is dead," as many have done and questioned why things weren't happening in my life when

Finding Faith

I wanted or as I wanted them to. "God if you told me to start my business, why do I not have any customers? And God if you called me to write why aren't the books selling?" I cried. I'm putting in the work, but nothing is working. Then I cried about not having a job and bills piling up . . . blah, blah, blah. Yes, I spent many nights crying!

Just because what God commanded you to do is not working as you thought it should, or is not what you want to do in the order you want to do it, will not make God change His mind. God always gives us instructions. We must follow, regardless of the outcome and regardless of whether we understand or not. These words still hurt, "You continue to ask me what to do, I continue to tell you to write, you are being disobedient." Ouch!

God gave us all gifts and talents. With purpose, He gave us instructions on how to use those gifts on the earth to benefit the kingdom.

The enemy uses pain and trials to make us throw our gifts aside and try to work out our problems on our own. But in order for what the devil meant for evil to be used for our good, we must learn to be consistent in using our gifts even during trials. Your job is to continue on the path and plan that God laid out. His job is to supply all your needs and fight your battles.

We must learn to be unstoppable. If you are not consistent now, how can God trust you to become dependable when you reach the Promised Land? Doors are closed because God wants you to use your gift and do what He has instructed you to do. He is silent because you are not doing what He told you to do.

I know the importance of my writing. I know what God has promised regarding my writing and my books. Yet in frustration I stop writing and allow days and even weeks to pass before I write again. Yet I expect God to still fulfill His part. All God's promises come with conditions. And the condition is you must do your part. This is the work that must exemplify your faith. God tells us what work to do, we cannot do what we want to do. You don't have to wonder what your part is or assume you will stumble across the correct path through trial and error.

God is a God of order. He reveals His plan, one step at a time. When one step is complete, the next will be revealed. If you do not know what to do, perhaps you are ignoring His instructions because it does not seem practical or logical according to your current situation. I certainly understand. It just does not seem logical to me to be writing books, while I have a mountain of bills and bill collectors calling me every other day. One thing I do know is that I serve a supernatural God, and therefore if it made logical sense, I wouldn't need His direction.

Working your faith, in the midst of turmoil, provides you with peace that surpasses all understanding. There is peace in knowing that you are obedient and therefore you can demand the promises of God. People don't like to use the word demand when referring to God. But obedience moves God. His word says, "test me and see." God's promises always proceed His commands. If you fulfill the command you can demand the promise. And in fulfilling the

You must exalt Him with your gift before He will exalt you in the earth.

command, you can be sure that you are ready for what you asked for. Because He whom God calls, He also prepares.

mess things up and the more you prevent God from moving in your life. You cannot have God's glory. Pride is a sneaky little devil. Celebrating your accomplishments is not the issue, rather it's the entitlement to the things of God that poses the problem.

Think of the five things or experiences that make you most proud. My five include my education, purchasing and renovating my home, writing a book and becoming an author, starting a business, and helping people get into college. I am very proud of my accomplishments. But because of my education, I felt I deserved a good job. Because I purchased and renovated my home, I labeled myself as the epitome of independence. Because I wrote a book, I felt I deserved to become a best seller. Because I started a business, I wanted it to prosper. Get my point. I expected to go higher and higher because of what I accomplished. It never occurred to me that I was attempting to exalt myself. I needed to allow God to make them prosper, in His timing, in His way, and my job was to submit. We are deserving because God chose us, not because of what we did.

Now think of your most embarrassing moments. Ironically, all my most embarrassing moments came during this period of unemployment. They included applying for food stamps, being unemployed, and asking others for money or help. While I am no stranger to using food stamps, it did something to my ego to have to go to the Department of Human Services, fill out the application, provide all my personal financial details, and actually receive a card in the mail with MY name on it! Sitting in that office I was terrified that one of my old clients would see me there. It did not matter that I had often told my clients, "don't be ashamed, we all need help sometimes." But not ME! I am Ms. Independent, I have been working my whole life, and I have never been without a job. Not only am I without a job, but I have to ask people for help and ask for money!

And He said unto me, "My grace is sufficient for you, for My strength is made perfect in weakness." Therefore most gladly I will rather boast in my infirmities, that the power of Christ may rest upon me.
—*2 Corinthians 12:9 (NKJV)*

In my weakness, God is exalted. If I had not been needy, how would I know that God would supply all my needs? If I had not been needy, how would I learn to trust God? Real service begins once we are humbled. If I could do it on my own, I would not need God. If God is not in it, it will never prosper nor benefit the kingdom. In our trials, God is building a foundation. A foundation of trust in Him, elimination of pride, and complete surrender cannot be broken.

Therefore whoever hears these sayings of Mine, and does them, I will liken him to a wise man who build his house on the rock; and the rain descended, the floods came, and the winds blew and beat on that house; and did not fall, for it was founded on the rock.
—*Matthew 7: 24-25 (NKJV)*

Sometimes you don't know you are standing on the rock, until after the storm passes. When the rain and floods wash away, the rock is still standing, you are safe. Yes your clothes are wet, hair is tussled and eyes bloodshot red, but you are standing. Sometimes we are not even aware that the rock is there, until the storm comes and we search for higher ground. We find that the rock is unmovable, steady, and all that we need. Once we experience the rock, after the storm has passed, we recognize its power and never step down. This is the intent and purpose we were meant to discover.

Let Go of Your Will

Sometimes even in our best efforts, we are no way closer to the knowledge of the things God has in store for us. Remember as I stated earlier, God only shows us pieces to the puzzle, rarely does He give us the entire picture. Why? Because in our humanness, in our inability to wait, in our avoidance of pain and in our desire for pleasure we would mess it up. Even though God reveals His purpose for us, as limited as it may be, the journey, the pain, the heartache, is often left out. When Joseph was dreaming about his family one day bowing to him, God did not mention the pit and false imprisonment. Therefore, when the trials come, the first thing the enemy tells us is that we have sinned or did something to cause our valley experience.

Faith knows that God is able and decides to obey regardless of the outcome.

Coming to Him as to a living stone, rejected indeed by man, but chosen by God and precious.

—1 Peter 2:4 (NKJV)

Though we may feel rejected when we are going through difficult times, faith is not about our feelings. Faith stands on the promises. Faith stands on the word despite adversity. Faith continues to declare, thus says the Lord. Faith rests in the lions' den. Faith knows regardless of how high the heat, it will not be consumed. During my struggles and trials, the Holy Ghost reminded me of Shadrach, Meshach, and Abednego in the fiery furnace. As I re-read the story, the Holy-Ghost asked me, "Where does it say they fought and resisted the fiery furnace?" Many times we try to avoid the heat, justifying doing so because of the favor of God. Truth is the favor of God, is the reason you are in the fire. Notice while they are in the fire, the bystanders see an angel in there with them. Notice that while they are in the fire, the scriptures do not mention any murmuring or complaining, or pleading or begging for God to intervene. In fact, they had already decided, before being thrown in, that God was able to save them and if He chose not to they were going to honor Him anyway. Notice also that when they came out, the King did not praise them, he praised their God. This is the ultimate goal of God. That the people will see His power and His faithfulness and praise Him, not you.

No one knows the outcome but God. But understand God will not be mocked. His word will not return to Him void. He will not allow you to be shamed or Him to be embarrassed for standing on His word.

Know that you are chosen and precious. If things are not going well . . . remember you are chosen! Doors closing? You keep hitting brick walls? . . . remember you are chosen! Regardless of the situation, you are chosen. God chose you to endure it. He chose you to bear it. He chose you to suffer for His namesake.

Finding Faith

Though you are in the fire, remember God is with you. You will not be consumed. Do not be concerned with the how and what is awaiting you when you come out: job, promotion, money, etc. Doing so only clouds your judgment and prevents you from seeing God's work. For in your coming out, God will be victorious, He will be glorified. All will praise His name. Stop concerning yourself with the why and when. His timing is perfect. Bask in His peace. Know that your faith shall fail you not.

Let Go of Your Expectations

Faith does not beg God for what He has already promised. Instead it remembers the word and stands therefore.

The mere foundation of faith is expecting God to do what He promised. But this is not the expectation we need to let go of. Yes, we are to expect the faithfulness of God. But we are not to expect Him to do it according to our knowledge and our understanding. In other words, stop trying to figure God out! Doing so prevents freedom of movement and control by the heavens. Doing so also hardens your heart and produces a spirit of ungratefulness.

Before I became unemployed I clearly heard God say He was going to give me a business and my books would bring healing to the nations. Fast forward 2 months into my unemployment and I am frustrated that I haven't found a job, nor been called in for an interview, and not to mention book sales were horrible. I launched my own business, created a website, placed a profile on Psychology today, handed out flyers, opened a business bank account, created a Facebook page and even placed ads on Facebook. No profits, no business revenue, I could not buy a vowel or even pay attention for that matter. Those who did respond wanted me to volunteer my services. I created a website for my books, created an author page on Amazon, emailed singles groups at local churches, sent out letters and free books to churches and bookstores, placed ads on Facebook, and purchased vendor booths at book events. No one responded to my letters, emails, or voicemails, and I sold no more than 10 books at events (not even making my money back). I even started applying for jobs at temp agencies, only to get a reply of "over qualified" or "no jobs available" in your field. Finally, around September I cried out to God, "Why is nothing working? I don't know what else to do!" His response was, "When did I tell you I needed your help?"

I was tiring myself out. I was trying to make God's promises happen through my own efforts. I was trying to speed up the process. I was trying to run through the wilderness. I was creating chaos and stress where God was giving me rest and peace. I was focusing on not having a job, not having money, not being able to pay all my bills and I neglected to see that God was providing for me. I may not have all I wanted but I had everything I needed.

Let Go of Your Timing

The word tells us there is a season and a time for everything.

Finding Faith

Yet why do we humor God by telling Him when enough is enough. Only the potter knows when enough heat has been applied to perfectly mold the clay into the object of his desire. Clay begins as a sticky mushy substance of infinite possibilities. But the potter comes along, with vision and a plan, applies heat and shapes the clay into a hard surface for a specific use.

Tell the truth and shame the devil! As Christians we want the world to think that following Christ is a life of luxury, success, and devoid of trouble. Truth is, we are embarrassed. Scratch that. Truth is, I was embarrassed. Here I am proclaiming to be believing God for a husband, a career, and becoming a great author and speaker; and the reality is I was unemployed, behind on bills, dodging creditors, had no money for food or gas, had lost my cable and internet, was in danger of losing my house, and the icing on this horrible cake was I lost my mother. I felt alone, helpless, hopeless and embarrassed. Why embarrassed? Because I believe in God for all those things, I encouraged others to go after their dreams, and here I am struggling and suffering. Nothing is happening and there was nothing I could do about it.

Why am I here? I live right. I go to church. I pay my tithes. I give my offerings. I help others. I did what He told me to do: I wrote the book, I did the work, I got my education, and I honored

Faith focuses on the timing of God's faithfulness rather than the time in the struggle.

my mother. The books are not selling, I still had no husband, no job, and my mother died! Why am I here? What did I do wrong? I'm tired and I don't know what else to do!

You see we think the storm, the trials and the heartaches are about us! In reality it's really about God. The enemy heard you say you believe in God. The enemy heard you tell God "Yes" to his will. The enemy heard you declare, "I will trust the Lord." Now it's time to put your money where your mouth is, it's time to put up or shut up. The devil wants you to curse God, to question His ability, to become frustrated in the wait, to get angry and lash out at God. But look at the big picture. The devil wants you to give up and turn your back on God. Yet God has faith in you! He knows what He put in you. He knows that the trials you are going through and your ability to ride out the storm, will benefit others. The devil is trying to destroy you, to stop your purpose. But God is building the kingdom, starting with you.

Why are you here? Trials come to test your faith. You will either fight or flee. Decide that the promises of God and your purpose are worth more than your current pain. Decide that you have come too far to give up. Decide that you have been through too much not to see this thing through. Decide that what you are believing in God for is better than what you can even imagine. Decide that despite the criticism, despite the feelings of shame or embarrassment, and despite the tiredness, that God cannot, will not, and did not lie! Look the devil right in the eye and decide that despite his best efforts you will not give up on God. Decide that the greatness you seek is worth the pain.

Faith does not mean that you will never cry or have a moment of weakness. I believe that God allows us to have our temporary moments of anger.

Be angry, and do not sin; do not let the sun go down on your wrath, nor give place to the devil.

—Ephesians 4: 26-27 (NKJV)

Cry, yell, stomp your feet, get mad at God... just don't stay there. Have your pity party, just remember to take down the decorations at the end of the day. I laugh every time I have my little temper tantrums because after a few hours or a few days (if I'm really upset), I hear the Holy Ghost say, "Are you done yet?" Sometimes with my spoiled, stubborn self I will say, "nope, a few more days." And in a few more days, I will hear Him again ask, "Are you done yet?" Then I will say, "Yes," and He will say, "Good, because we have work to do."

Faith does not allow frustrations during the trial to cause a reaction that will be detrimental to the future.

Remember that you have work to do. Remember that purpose is driving. Remember it is only temporary. Stop working so hard to make things happen and let God do it for you. Don't be distracted by your own needs instead allow God to manifest His plan in you. Don't do anything. You will burn yourself out. Sometimes our pain and suffering is caused by defensive wounds. We are trying to fight physically what can only be fought spiritually. God has already shown you. Trust His timing. Trust His power. Remember that if He allowed it, He has a purpose for it.

The enemy wants to throw you off course, but God wants to make you unstoppable.

Know That You Are Not Alone

But may the God of all grace, who called us to His eternal glory by Christ Jesus, after you have suffered a while, perfect, establish, strengthen, and settle you.

—1 Peter 5: 10 (NKJV)

You are not alone. Loneliness is a trick of the enemy. God is with you and His word promises that He will never leave you. Know that your suffering is not in vain. You are being perfected. You are being established. You are being strengthened. You are being settled. All for His perfect will and His glory. His grace is sufficient. His peace surpasses all understanding. Rest! Stop fighting, you can't change it or speed up the process.

Surrender. Realize you cannot do it by yourself. You cannot do it in your own strength. You would mess it up. Trials strengthen us and prepare us for the promises of God. Know that behind every success story is a testimony of great trials and tribulations.

Surrender. Accept God's perfect plan. It doesn't feel good now, but His plan is perfect. Accept that His plan IS greater, better, and far more beneficial than yours. Accept that your thoughts are not His thoughts. Accept that He only wants and has what's best for you.

Surrender. Realize it's not about you. It's not your battle.

Finding Faith

This fight is between God and the enemy. You are just a vessel. There is no victim in victory. You are more than a conqueror. Remember you cannot lose with God on the forefront.

Surrender. Accept God's timing is perfect. Regardless of how it hurts, bottom line is, God's appointed time has not come. But trust that the harder the storm, the closer you are to your destiny. Hold on to God.

CHAPTER SEVEN
In the Shadow of the Almighty

Faith is assurance in God's faithfulness to perform His word.

The word tells us and we often quote it, almost unconsciously, "God won't put more on us than we can handle." However, the fact is, we don't know what we can handle until we actually face it.

From the outside looking in, every situation seems manageable. But when heart break, unemployment, death, etc., knocks on your door, it knocks it off the hinges. We ball up on the floor in a fetal position screaming, "why is this happening to me?" or "what did I do wrong?"

It's easy to wallow in regret, shame, disappointment, fear, doubt etc., when life knocks the wind out of you. The storm is raging, the waters are rising, the fire is blazing and we have nowhere to turn except inward. Pity, defeat, despair, depression, etc., creep in. The devil doesn't fight fair, he tries to hit below the belt and kicks even harder when you're down. I now understand the meaning of "when it rains, it pours." Just when you think the storm is ceasing, something else happens. That something else for me was the death of my mother. But something else happened. Something the devil did not intend. God gave me a double blessing.

I had prayed for her healing. I asked God to allow me to see her walk and take care of herself again. I asked Him to remove the pain and give her back her joy. But when the news of her death came to me. I froze for a moment, then I felt a lifting. I could not explain it at the moment. I even tried to discount the feeling. I told myself, your mother just passed, you should be sad and hurt. As I headed to the hospital, I began to question God. But when I walked into that hospital room, Sept 26, 2015 and saw her lying in that bed, I could not cry! She was glowing. At first, I said to myself it was the illumination from the light over her head. But it was an internal glow, she looked so good. She was at peace. How could I be mad at God for that?

Later that night, as I lay alone in my bed. I went through the pictures in her phone and began to wail before the Lord. I cried out, "God you were supposed to heal her not take her!" His reply was, "I did heal her and I also delivered you." You see the lifting I felt, was the lifting of all the hurt, pain and anger I felt regarding my past. Because of my hurt I was unable to see the beauty of the mother God blessed me with.

Whenever I came into her presence, though I took care of her, the memories of the molestation, physical abuse, alcohol and drug abuse, and verbal abuse I either witnessed or was victimized by came flooding back. But in that moment, I remembered the bad times no more. The good memories of my childhood, that I thought did not exist or I just could not remember, came flooding back. That night my brother and I spent two hours on the phone texting, sending pictures and talking about the good ole days.

Finding Faith

As the days passed guilt tried to set in, regarding me not being there for her last days in the hospital. But God reminded me that He makes no mistakes. He reminded me that He honored me in all my requests. A few years ago, when I often prayed for my mother's salvation, God told me He was going to save her and then He was going to take her. I kind of brushed it off. But in May 2015 when my brother was released from prison, God told me again, "she won't be with you too much longer." I remember telling my brother what God had said, one night when we were at the hospital with her.

This last year was very hard on my mother. She was in and out of the hospital. On top of dialysis, diabetes, and high blood pressure, she experienced a herniated disk and staph infection that left her unable to walk and care for herself. She had to come live with me for a few months. Dialysis left her weak, and they soon diagnosed her with congestive heart failure. I watched my mother in severe pain for the last year and a half. I am grateful that God gave me the opportunity to fix my relationship with her. I even asked Him not to take her at home, because I felt I would not be able to handle discovering her body. God reminded me that He honored my every request. I watched her accept Him as her Lord and Savior one Sunday at my church, I watched her cry out to the Lord for saving her and asked him to watch over her babies.

The last week leading up to her death she had some interesting conversations with my brother and me. She told my brother where to find her insurance papers. She made us both promise to be there and take care of each other. I remember sitting on the edge of her bed and telling her "Mom, the Lord said just a little while longer, hold on." And her response was, "I hope so because I'm tired of hurting." She was ready. I did not like to see her in pain. Though I would have loved for her to be with us a little while longer. I would rather her be with God in perfect peace and strength, than to be here with me in pain. That peace and strength is what illuminated her body, when I walked into her hospital room. I saw her as the strong, stubborn, outspoken woman I knew her to be growing up.

My mother taught me to be strong, to be a survivor, to "never let'em see you sweat." I realized that we fought so much because we were just alike. Yes, I am stubborn, outspoken and strong as well. It took her death for me to realize all these years we were both fighting for the same thing. She was hard on me, because she didn't want me to go through the pain she went through and she wanted better for me. I was so busy fighting to not be like her, that I didn't realize that it is her strength that I needed to make it through the storms life sent my way.

The devil didn't plan for me to be at peace with my mother's death. He wanted me to wallow in guilt and regret. But God had another plan. God prepared me. He allowed me time to get it right. He gave me this time of unemployment to honor and care for her. He allowed me to witness her ultimate healing. He gave me what I asked for. I told God I would be ok as long as I knew she was with Him. He allowed me to

> *Faith seeks out God's peace when storms come. It does not allow the enemy to keep it in darkness because it recognizes it is surrounded by light.*

witness her salvation. I smile now when I remember her fussing at me or complaining about me not doing what she wanted me to do.

This is the message which we have heard from Him and declare to you, that God is light and in Him is no darkness at all. If we say that we have fellowship with Him, and walk in darkness, we lie and do not practice the truth.

—*1 John 1: 5-6 (NKJV)*

Even in the hard times, we have to believe and trust that God makes no mistakes. His way is perfect. His timing is perfect. Doubt casts a shadow of darkness around you. Remove the doubt. Open your heart and allow God's glory to manifest its perfect peace. Our thoughts and speech continue to keep us in darkness. We must stop allowing the enemy to torment our thoughts.

Rest in His shadow. You are protected. His peace surpasses all understanding. You may be justified in your pity but it is not good for you, and God does not come to our pity parties.

The hardest thing for me to do during this season was to stop fighting. I still don't know if I have completely stopped. Letting go is very difficult, especially when the world tells us to try, try again. Try harder. Pull yourself up by your own boot straps. You are the master of your own destiny. Truth is, as God's children, we cannot live by the world's standards. The word tells us to take up our cross and follow him. In order to follow Christ, we must first die to self. We have to give up our wants and desires for His will and purpose. This season is teaching me to be totally dependent on God, rely on His direction, and to blindly follow whether I understand or whether it feels good.

Sometimes we spend time trying to fight our own battles and wonder why nothing is working out. We attempt to run through the wilderness, not realizing we are running in circles, because God decides when the wilderness time has ended.

Life will be much easier the sooner you stop trying to assist Him. We must realize that what God has for us is better and greater than we can even imagine. God told me that what I was waiting for is minuscule to what He was actually going to do. He just needed me to trust Him. He wanted me to do nothing! I went against what God said, because it did not seem logical and it actually caused me more stress and anxiety. God told me to write. Yet I spent time applying for jobs, everywhere. I have applied for over 120 jobs in the last ten months. Every email and letter, proclaiming, "though your skills were impressive we have decided to go with a candidate more suited for our current business needs," ate at my self-esteem and confidence. I began to question my abilities and even my purpose. I would tell others, God told me to write, not look for a job, and they would reply "you need a job, while you wait for God to open a door in your writing." So, I kept applying and kept getting frustrated and disappointed. I was confused. I didn't understand why God had not intervened and opened a door in my employment search though I was facing losing everything.

Again, I heard God say, "I gave you this time to write." The fear of losing material things kept me fighting. Anything that you lose following God, He will give you double for your trouble. What was I really losing? Yeah, I'm behind on my bills, but they can't repossess anything. Everything in my house is paid for. My car is paid for. As I put my house up for short sale, God reminded me that He has something better.

It's not your battle! Your works are not productive because God wants you to rest. In order to rest in the shadow of the Almighty, we have to remember that He always wins.

Remember Job. God offered him up to Satan for testing. Satan's reply was (in my own words), "I've tried but you have a hedge of protection around him." God removed the hedge but instructed Satan that he could not touch his person. Realize that though the storm is raging, though it seems unbearable, it cannot and will not kill you. The magnitude of the storm does not matter, as long as you realize that God is with you. Again, it's not about you. It's about the people you will help with your testimony.

The testing of your faith is not about the magnitude of the storm but about your ability to keep your eyes on Jesus.

You Are Covered

Repeat after me, "God's got me, He is working it out." Satan intensifies the storm so that we can forget that we are not alone. So that we can become frustrated, engulfed with fear, and overwhelmed with shame, and slip into depression. All of which leads to lack of communication with God, lack of praying, failure to fellowship with like believers, procrastination or giving up completely. The word tells us to abide in Him and He will abide in us. The reward is that He will give us the desires of our heart. Not because we deserve it but because as we develop a closer relationship with Him, His thoughts become our thoughts, His ways become our ways. We begin to desire what He desires for us. God speaks frequently but He speaks through His word. We cannot make it through the storm, we cannot dwell in His shadow without praying and reading the word.

To stop fighting does not mean to do nothing. It does not mean that you just stand there and take it. It means that you cast all your cares on Him. It means that you recognize that this is a spiritual battle rather than a physical one. It means that you diligently seek Him daily. Don't just tell God how bad the storm is, He already knows that, He is in the storm with you. Proclaim the word and declare His promises over the situation.

Faith expects victory and decrees, regardless of the test, that the enemy will not win.

Stop focusing on the storm, what we focus on we tend to magnify. When we focus on the storm, we worry about when it will be over, and how God will do it. Faith knows we are victorious in the end. However, God's timing is not our timing. Worrying will not speed up God's time, rather it prolongs the time.

Rather than focus on the fact that I have been out of work nearly a year. The Holy Spirit pointed out God has been providing for a whole year. What if you are reaping what you sowed?

Finding Faith

What if you are being punished? What if God is upset with you? So what! Repent and get back on track. Don't allow the enemy to keep you wallowing in regret. Christians are quick to quote the part of the scripture that says, "God will make a way of escape," but fail to acknowledge the part that says, "that you are able to bear it." Crying, "get me out Jesus," does not work. You must learn to bear it. You cannot bear it alone. Running solves nothing. Just ask Jonah.

I have written to you fathers, because you have known Him who was from the beginning. I have written to you, young men, because you are strong, and the word of God abides in you, and you have overcome the wicked one.
—1 John 2:14 (NKJV)

God chastises those He loves. You are strong. Rely on your strength, stop trying to hide it. People are watching. Your strength is seen by everyone but you. Fear creates weak thoughts and that weakness prevents you from basking in God's presence, in His peace, in His shadow. Stop viewing yourself, your circumstances through world view. Stop speaking and acting as you think the world wants you to speak. God chose you, because you know the word and He is in you. Hold your head up. Your joy is in the Lord. Isn't it better to go through with God than without Him? You have no reason to be sad, to be embarrassed, or to be shamed. The more you speak about the storm the more you are allowing it to control your happiness.

You are covered. Bask in His strength. Stop seeking sympathy and confirmation from man. God has already told you. Perhaps you were not aware of the storms coming or its magnitude. But with greatness comes opposition. The moment you accepted your calling and decided to pursue your purpose, the enemy declared war on you.

You are covered. God has not forgotten you. Never forget that you are not alone. Relax in His presence. In His presence there is fullness of joy. You can either choose to worry or choose to give it to God. You cannot do both. Worry produces doubt and God cannot work where there is doubt. Guard your eyes and your heart. Watch what you watch on TV, listen to on the radio, and the amount of time spent on mindless activity. Human nature wants to escape, to take our mind off of our situation. Escape in the word, with prayer and meditation on the goodness of the Lord.

You are covered. Satan is on a leash. Everything he does he must get permission. Therefore, if God allowed, He has a purpose for it. Stop trying to figure it out. In due season, at the appointed time, you will fully understand.

> *Faith knows heaven is rejoicing at its ability to stand.*

Wait for God

And now, little children, abide in Him that when He appears, we may have confidence and not be ashamed before Him at His coming.

—*1 John 2:28 (NKJV)*

Finding Faith

Faith is confidence in God's coming and is strengthened as you abide in Him. Faith is not manifested out of God's presence.

They are tossed to and fro and are unable to withstand the storm. Some tests do not come with a pass or fail and repeat but rather stand, trust, and believe.

Faith is about knowing that God is able. The myth is that faith always has a victorious outcome. This is partly true but he who exhibits faith is not necessarily the one who will enjoy its benefits. Aren't we glad that Abraham stood the test of faith? He did not live to see all His descendants. Aren't we glad that Mary and Joseph stood the test of faith? They probably did not fully understand the magnitude of their sacrifice. We are still benefiting from the sacrifices of the great men and women of faith. Faith knows that God will whether they see it or not. Faith is about the kingdom not one specific individual.

Faith is manifested through communication and relationship with God.

Faith is the realization of God's strength, power and faithfulness. His strength to carry you through the storm. His power to defeat the enemy. His faithfulness to perform His word. We must learn to wait "For" God regardless of what it feels like, what it looks like, or what others think or say. There is a difference in waiting "on" God and waiting "for" God:

> To wait **"on"** (upon) God is to await His assistance while serving and working. God

will usually give instructions of what to do during the wait to serve Him and others. Such as waiting for Him to fulfill a promise such as marriage, childbirth, etc.

To wait **"for"** God is to remain or rest in expectation to look forward to confidently. Waiting for God is to await His instruction before moving. Such as awaiting the next step in a journey, you cannot move until He speaks.

The two can seem confusing. Waiting on God requires an appointed time set by God for the promise to manifest. While waiting for God requires a series of events to happen. Neither of which is known by the one waiting. Either way we must stay close to Him to make it through. For without Him, we will get weary in well-doing and become frustrated in the wait.

The myth of faith is that it always requires action on our part. This is true to a certain extent but we cannot confuse the working of our faith with trying to help God out. Attempting to help God out can cause excess damage during the storm and can even prolong the storm. As with the children of Israel, sometimes all that's required in the working of our faith is trusting and believing God and standing on those promises regardless of the storm.

Don't Focus on the Storm

Don't be so focused on the storm that you forget you are weathering it. The trick of the enemy is to keep you so stressed, so worried, so frustrated, that you forget that God is in the storm with you. Once you realize that God is in the boat with you, the degree of the storm should no longer matter. Why?

Finding Faith

Because it cannot overtake you. Learn to rest in His care. Rest because the complaining only makes a mountain out of a mole hill.

Learn to dance in the rain. Remember God is your joy. Remember the enemy wants to take your mind off God and onto your problems. Dancing in the rain is similar to a kid being stuck in the house due to bad weather but eventually finding other ways to amuse himself. Day one of the bad weather, the kid may be moping around the house, bored and complaining that there is nothing to do. But by day 2 the kid is eating up all the food, bouncing on furniture, writing on walls, playing games, etc., and the parent is praying, "Lord please let the storm cease so this kid can get outside!" I'm convinced video games were invented by someone stuck in the house during bad weather. Adversity brings out the best in us, without it some of us would never reach our destiny. Don't get me wrong you are not to get comfortable in the storm either, but you are to rest in confidence knowing that the rain will cease in due time.

Remember rain helps things grow. In order for your faith to grow, the rain has to come.

As humans if we get tired of hearing other's problems, don't you think God gets tired of hearing about the magnitude of the storms in our lives? As soon as the rain starts, the complaining and the professions of our tiredness begins. God knows who you will be and what you will be when you come out. Trust His plan. As long as we belong to Jesus and live a life of holiness, the devil can do nothing in our lives without God's permission. If God allowed it, He has a purpose for it. As long as you are complaining, you are unable to see its purpose.

Don't focus on the storm, because just as a watched clock never moves, a watched storm never ceases. Instead praise God that you are making it through. Thank God that your life is in His hands. Rest in confidence, knowing that your steps are ordered by God. Rest in hope, knowing that nothing can overtake you that God has not already equipped you to handle.

Don't focus on the storm, because doing so gives glory to the enemy. Instead focus on the victory. Focus on the fact that the word says you are more than a conqueror. Remember that all things work together for the good of those who love the Lord and are called according to His purpose. Remember His promises, remember that what He promised shall come to pass. Focus on the testimony that will follow and those that you will help.

Don't focus on the storm because it is not about you. It's bigger than you. It's about purpose. Many forget that purpose is not selfish. Your purpose, your anointing, your gift, is for the kingdom, for God's people. Above all, you are a servant. God's great commission to all followers of Christ is to spread the good news. The good

Faith is assurance in God's faithfulness to perform His word and His promises.

Finding Faith

news is that God loves, cares and is concerned for us all. And that He sent Jesus to free us from bondage. Your gift is to be used to set others free. If your intention does not include that, such as money, fame, etc., it's not going to work. The purpose of your storm may be to remove your selfish motivations.

In order to rest in His shadow, we must embrace and accept His control over our lives and His faithfulness. If you are unable to rest:

1. Examine yourself. Is there any sin that is causing you guilt and shame that you need to repent for? Ask for forgiveness and get back on track.
2. Are you trying to figure God out? God's ways are not our ways and His thoughts are not our thoughts. Rather than trying to figure out how He will do something, just rest knowing that He will.
3. Are you trying to help God out? Rather than keep running into brick walls or closed doors, ask God what He wants you to do and wait for His instructions. Do what He says, don't add to it. Remember if you could do it, you wouldn't need God.
4. Do you believe you are worthy? God determines our worth, not our works. Remember it is not you but rather the power of God in you that is able to do what God called you to do. Acknowledge God in all your ways and allow Him to direct your path. Remember God is a gentleman, He will not take over the reins of your life unless you let Him.
5. Eliminate fear. Don't fear. As you begin to recognize and bask in God's love, fear will cease.

There is no fear in love, but perfect love casts out all fear, because fear

involves torment. But he who fears has not been made perfect in love.
—1 John 4:18

Don't focus on the possibility of failure. With God there is no failure and He cannot operate in fear. Understand that God loves you. He has what is best for you. In His perfect love, He is making you fearless. He is taking you to the next level. The next move, you must be courageous. You must trust Him. You must abide in Him. The success you seek is in Him. Rely on Him. Depend on Him. He is all you ever needed. God's plans will be strategic. His directions will be clear. Do not question, move and go at His command. Perfect love casts out all doubt. Know that He loves you. The storm is not an indication of anger or disappointment towards you. It is to strengthen you for the next phase. You are not forgotten. God is always working. He never stopped working. Remember that soon you will understand and soon you will be enlightened.

Don't focus on the storm. Stay in His shadow. Fight for His presence. Pray harder. Read the bible more. Fellowship with like believers more. Give the enemy no room to squeeze in doubt and fear. Focus on the promises. Remember the words spoken over you. Write them down, read them every day. This is a spiritual fight. Stop trying to fight physically, you will tire yourself out. Rest in His word and the storm shall not consume you.

CHAPTER EIGHT
When Mourning Comes

Faith knows that loss is necessary to move from one season to the next, from glory to glory.

Mama was mean. There really is no better way to say it. I remember telling myself at 19, as I was moving out, "I'm glad to finally be out and I'm never coming back." She was always tough on me. I couldn't date or hang out with my friends. When everyone was at the mall hanging out or going to the movies, I had to stay home. I spent many nights alone in my room, crying myself to sleep, reading a book, studying or eating and watching television. At 14, I had my first boyfriend, behind my mother's back of course. I remember one night she came home, I couldn't have been no more than 15 or 16, and caught us lying naked in my bed asleep. I should have known better, my mother usually stayed out late, but no matter what time she came home, whether midnight or 3 a.m. she would always peek in my room and make sure I was ok. This night was no different. She peeked in my room and I guess she did a double take, because she peeked in, closed the door, then kicked it open about five seconds later. She started yelling and cursing, told him to get up and get out. Then she turned to me and said, "Get up and go take a bath you little whore." I never saw her the same again from that day forward. He and I continued to date throughout high school, I took a many beatings and tongue lashings for getting caught cutting school with him. I didn't care, she never understood me, and I felt like he was the only one who loved me.

Our relationship was tough. My adult years were spent trying to prove how grown up I was. I had my own place, I no longer had to listen to her cursing me out or calling me names. I made my own rules, and rule number one, "if you don't have anything nice to say, don't call me." I was always a sensitive child, up until I discovered boys, I didn't get many spankings. All she had to do was yell at me and I would go to bed crying. But her words stuck with me always. I remember feeling that life was unfair, that I had to take care of her when the drugs, alcohol and poor eating took its toll and lead to diabetes, high blood pressure and eventually dialysis and heart failure. I remember asking God why I had to take care of someone who never took care of me? Grudgingly, I did it. With no car, I had to take her to the grocery store, to pay bills, to doctor appointments, and even to see her mother and siblings when she wanted. I certainly wasn't happy about it, and neither was she, we couldn't be in each other's presence 10 minutes without arguing.

Sick and Tired of Being Sick and Tired

Around 2006, I rededicated my life to Christ and got back in church. Though I was changing, my mother reminded me how I couldn't possibly be a Christian and treat her the way that I did.

Finding Faith

One day, I finally admitted to God, she was right. How could I call myself a Christian, knowing the word says honor thy mother and thy father, and yet have so much anger and resentment against my own mother? I was angry but my mother was ill and it would have been selfish of me to express my anger at such an inopportune time. But I didn't know what to do with the anger. I was mad that all the ugly words she said to me over the years still rung in my ears like it was yesterday. I was mad that she didn't recognize the affects the molestations had on me. I was mad that the drugs and alcohol caused her to be present but absent. I was mad that I never knew my real father. I was mad that my life was not going the way I had planned. Yes, she was mean, but I was mad that though I tried hard not to, I was becoming just like her.

Rather than continuing to dwell in my anger, I began to pray for her salvation, and asked God to help me with my feelings and show me how to forgive. It wasn't easy, though I made many mistakes along the way, I learned to shut up! I stopped fighting her. But I was still wounded and spent many nights crying. I was even mad at God because He wouldn't let me defend myself. One day while on a mission trip with my church in 2008, I clearly heard God say he was going to save her and then he was going to take her. But He needed me to show her Him.

Faith is allowing God to shine a light into the darkest of places.

Indiana Tuggle

As I stated earlier, it wasn't until May 2015 that I heard God speak those words again. My brother was returning home from prison and we went to meet him at the bus station. As she limped over to greet and hug him, smile as wide as the Pacific Ocean, I heard the Lord say, "Not too much longer." At first, I didn't think anything of it, but a week later as I spoke with my brother on the phone, I told him what I heard God say. The next few months were very hard on her. She was in and out of the hospital, broke her ankle in six places, couldn't walk and could barely take care of herself. But she was one tough cookie, she wanted to stay in her home, and I came over two to three times a week to cook food and make sure she took her medicine. Each time before I left I would pray and God would always tell me to tell her, "hold on, not too much longer."

I replayed the days leading to her death over and over in my mind a thousand times. Why wasn't I there with her when she went to the hospital? Why didn't I answer the phone when she called begging me to come check on her because she wasn't feeling well? Why didn't I go see her in the hospital the day before? She went to dialysis three days a week on Tuesdays, Thursdays and Saturdays. Tuesday night when she came home from dialysis she wasn't feeling well and called me to come over. I went over and fixed dinner, helped her take a bath, and kissed her good night. Again that night I prayed and said, "Mama, God said hold on, just a little while longer." But this time she responded, "I hope so, because I'm tired." Thursday night, she got back from dialysis and wasn't feeling well again. She called me, but I was tired and didn't feel like being bothered. I didn't answer. The next morning, she called me from the hospital and told me she was admitted the night before because her chest was hurting and she was throwing up, but that she was feeling better now. I informed her that I was taking my brother to handle some business and would be by to see her. "Don't bother," she said, "just take care of your brother and y'all can come see me in the morning, I'm fine." That night I went to my 20-year high school reunion. The next morning, I called her room about 10 a.m. to let her know I was on the way. No answer. I called my grandmother to see if she had heard anything. She informed me that she had spoken with her a few minutes earlier and that they were taking her down for tests and then off to dialysis. "Cool," I thought. I can go a little later when she finishes dialysis. Dialysis normally takes about four hours, so I decided to go to our Alumni picnic but would leave early and spend the evening with my mother. At about 4 p.m. as I stood in line at the picnic for fried fish, a childhood acquaintance tapped me on the shoulder and said, "Ain't you Dell's daughter?" "Yes," I said. "Somebody just posted on Facebook that she died!" My heart dropped.

She always told me I would miss her when she was gone. I never knew how true that statement was until I saw the glow on her face when I walked into that hospital room. At that moment I finally saw what God saw. A woman at peace. A woman who had been beaten and bruised. A woman victimized by false love. A woman finally embraced by the one who loved her most. Still unable to cry I covered her feet with a blanket, because she was always cold, and leaned down to kiss her cheeks and whispered softly in her ear, "Rest in peace sister girl."

Questioning God

That night I battled with God for not allowing me to say

goodbye, for not enabling me to release my anger sooner, for not allowing her to hear me say I loved her one last time. I yelled, screamed, tossed, turned, and then finally closed my eyes. I sunk into my bed, frozen with peace. This moment felt familiar. I remember this touch. I felt it 25+ years ago, I was about 13 or so. I don't remember what happened that day that left me so distraught. But I remember the knife in my hand, going back and forth over my wrist. I remember the tears burning my cheeks. I remember rocking and crying, uttering, "Nobody loves me, nobody cares." By the time those words slid out of my mouth the third time. I heard Him say, "I love you." I knew it was Him, because it wasn't the first time I'd heard Him. I recalled that voice from when I was eight years old, the year I was molested and was bullied every day at school. My teacher saw such anguish in my eyes and witnessed the change in behavior that she gave me a diary. That night, sitting up in my bed, rocking and tears flowing, I began to write, "Nobody loves me, nobody cares. Why do they hate me?" That night was the first time I heard Him say, "I love you." At eight, I turned over, cuddled my diary and cried myself to sleep. At 13, I put the knife down, cuddled my pillow and cried myself to sleep. Now at 38, I took a deep breath, cuddled my pillow, and cried myself to sleep. Again, God came to my rescue, again He heard my cry, again He embraced me with His love and gave me peace.

    I remember lying there, resting in His arms in His presence and telling God, "But I have no good memories, I can't remember the good times." At that moment the phone rang. It was my brother. He and I began talking about our childhood and the years we spent in Texas. And the memories came back like a flood. I remembered our first days of school, the first

Finding Faith

snow day in Texas in years and us sliding down the street on cardboard. I remembered our first Christmas when I got the cabbage patch doll and roller skates I wanted. I remembered the year my father left and went back to Memphis, my mother wanted us to have a good Christmas but she couldn't afford the doll house I wanted but she got me all of the furniture instead. My brother and I went to the school and got 6 milk crates. I stacked them in the corner of my room two by two and decorated them with my new furniture. I remembered how every Saturday she would get up and cook buffet style breakfast and afterwards we would sit at the table and play monopoly. That is probably why breakfast is my favorite meal. It all came back at that moment. We stayed on the phone until the sun came up. I remember finally crying myself to sleep but this time it was tears of joy.

> *Faith is allowing the word to do the work.*

And God will wipe away every tear from their eyes; there shall be no more death, nor sorrow, nor crying. There shall be no more pain, for the former things have passed away.
—*Revelation 21:4*

In that moment, in a matter of hours God took away 25 years of anger and blame. That night changed my whole perspective of my childhood and my mother. I no longer saw a mean woman taking her anger and shortcomings out on me. I saw a mother, beaten down at the hands of men who said they loved her, entrapped by drugs and alcohol, trying to make sure her kids had a better life than she had. I saw a woman who didn't know how to be a mother but did the best she could. I saw a woman God chose as a vessel to bring me into this world. There was something she had that I needed. I needed her strength. Her ability to endure great pain was passed down to me and enabled me to endure the blows that life had for me. Perhaps some would say she choose the wrong path which led to the drugs and alcohol, but she also chose to stay. She stayed, she could have aborted us, she could have abandoned us, and she could have left us with my aunts or grandmother to raise. But she stayed, took responsibility and most importantly she introduced us to God. Though I never saw her go to church growing up, she made sure we went. When the church van came into the neighborhood, she put me on that bus. And for that I am grateful!

When will it end?

No sooner than we buried my mother, another storm was brewing. During this time, I was unemployed, the unemployment checks ended a few months earlier and I was overwhelmed with grief, I was also stressed out over the possibility of losing my house. I even started smoking. One day, while standing on the porch smoking a cigarette, I heard the Lord say, "Let it go." "But God, you gave me this house," I said. "Let it go, I have better," He said. I went back inside, called my mortgage company and started the short sale procedures. My house sold in 1 week. We had a buyer and proof of funds before the mortgage company had received all the paperwork and approved the short sale. Approximately 30 days later, the bank approved and my brother and I had 45 days to move. With no job and no income, I could not qualify for an apartment. Luckily my brother found a private homeowner willing to lease to us. It wasn't the best neighborhood, but it was a roof.

I did not have the strength to pack. It was the weekend before we had to move and my brother asked me, "Are you going to pack?" I responded, "We have another week." He was like, "Sis we have to be out Monday." I had completely lost track of days and time. I went to the kitchen to start packing and had an anxiety attack. My chest began to tighten, I couldn't breathe, and I started to wobble from the light headedness. My brother caught me, lead me back to my room and said, "I got it Sis." Here I thought I was helping him by giving him a place to stay as he returned home from prison, and it turns out he was helping me. As we moved into the new place, regret and guilt moved in with me.

Beloved, do not think it strange concerning the fiery trial which is to try you, as though some strange thing happened to you; but rejoice to the extent that you partake of Christ's sufferings, that when His glory is revealed, you may also be glad with exceeding joy.

—1 Peter 4: 12 - 13

I didn't have joy, I wasn't glad, and I did think it strange. What did I do to deserve this? I was a good girl, a good person, a good Christian. I went to church and paid my tithes. Why am I here? How is it that I lost so much in so little time, my job, my mom, and my house all in the same year! Depression snuck in through the window, and wreaked havoc. I slept all day and cried all night. I saw my mother's face when I closed my eyes and my house when I opened them. Not to mention the added stress of bill collectors calling daily. I couldn't pray, I couldn't write, I couldn't even explain what was happening. I was ashamed. Me, who wrote and talked about the goodness and faithfulness of the Lord, was going through hardship.

Every idle word I had spoken to my mother, every request she made and I said no when I could have said yes, every phone call I ignored, every opportunity I missed to simply have dinner with her, and the thought of her being in that hospital alone on her last days replayed in my mind every day, all day. The tears rolling down her face and the pain in her eyes were etched in my brain. I heard her voice calling me "Baby Girl," when she was just calling to say hello, "India" when she was expressing how proud she was of me, or "Nene," when she was angry at me.

I regretted not being there for her when I should have. I regretted making her cry. I regretted allowing my anger to prevent me from getting to know her. I didn't know her hopes, her dreams, or her pain. I never heard the stories of the experiences she had. I never sat at her feet and gleaned the wisdom in her years. How could she have known that I loved her when I didn't want to be in her presence?

So this I say, and affirm together with the Lord, that you walk no longer just as the Gentiles also walk, in the futility of their mind, being darkened in their understanding, excluded from the life of God because of the ignorance

Finding Faith

that is in them, because of the hardness of their heart;
—Ephesians 4:17-18

I allowed my anger to harden my heart. I was so busy being mad at who she wasn't, I didn't get a chance to know who she was. One conversation, one I'm sorry, one yes ma'am, could have changed the whole trajectory of our relationship and we were both too stubborn to say it.

I believe that my wanting to break free, wanting to mend our relationship, and wanting to honor God's word started the process of softening my heart. But I was not completely healed. As I stated before I didn't know what to do with the hurt. I did not know how to let go. I felt justified in my anger. I thought I had more time. I hoped that God would change her. I hoped that she would miraculously know what she had done wrong and apologize. The anger festered and bitterness grew.

When mourning comes, the hurt that won't allow you to forgive will be the same hurt that fuels your guilt. The pain of what could have been lay heavily upon your chest like a 3000-pound weight. And though the pain tightens upon your chest with every tear and with every restless night spent tossing and turning, the thought of the weight being removed causes more anguish. Thoughts of, "You don't deserve peace," play over and over in your head like a broken record that you refuse to get up and remove from the record player.

When mourning comes, the memories that fuel your anger will be the same memories that ignite your regret. What happened will be drowned out by the possibilities of what could have been. As the wasted time of yesterday ticks away at today, depression becomes a welcomed companion in your bed of misery. Though you yearn for sleep, sleep too is haunted by the inability, yet desperation to say, "I'm sorry."

When mourning comes the reality of never being able to see, touch, smell, talk to, or even argue with your loved one comes in waves like the ocean. The lost interactions, the missed moments and the drastic change in routine, leaves you in a state of bewilderment for days, weeks, even months after. The smallest or simplest of things that you took for granted, now flash in your mind like lights on an ambulance.

When mourning comes as quickly as a blink of an eye, you must fight to remember that God does not make mistakes. Though we don't understand grief or loss, He is still in control. You must fight to remember that it is perfectly ok to grieve, to cry, and to even feel guilt and regret. Even Jesus wept, knowing that He would raise Lazarus from the dead. I believe He wept not because of personal sadness or grief, but because of the compassion and the empathy He had for His friends in pain. He wept because of the temporary hopelessness that loss brings, even though we have hope standing before us waiting to embrace us with open arms.

To everything there is a season, A time for every purpose under heaven: A time to be born, and a time to die; a time to plant, and a time to pluck what is planted; a time to kill, and a time to heal; a time to break down, and a time to build up; a time to weep, and a time to laugh; a time to mourn, and a time to dance;

—*Ecclesiastes 2: 1-4*

Finding Faith

God ordained a time for everything, even mourning. However just as seasons change, mourning is not supposed to last forever. At some point your tears should turn to laughter, your sorrow into joy, and your pain into power. At some point your uncomfortable memories should be replaced with happy thoughts celebrating the life you shared rather than the times you missed. Grief awakens the Spirit man and sparks spiritual warfare because discomfort sends the flesh into darkness, a place where the Spirit man refuses to dwell. Because the love you shared is so strong, the flesh actually feels guilty and justifies sitting in the dark. In the dark you can replay those memories over and over. In the dark you can celebrate the day of their death every year. In the dark you can acknowledge them on every passing holiday. Remembering your loved one is not the issue, the refusal to let go and move on is the problem.

Moving on means no longer allowing the anniversary of their death or birthday to cause sorrow and pause in your life. Moving on means enjoying the moment and celebrating your successes without acknowledging their absence. If the enemy can keep you speaking, "I wish so and so were here," it prevents God from blessing you. Why? Because they can't be there, and hoping for someone to take part in something when God has said no is going against His will

Faith knows He has many more things in store, but they cannot come to pass if we are stuck on who and what we lost yesterday.

and questioning His plan. God doesn't take people and things away from us to hurt us or for us to dwell on what we once had.

CHAPTER NINE
New Beginnings

Faith does not always understand the road traveled but it trusts in the one leading. Faith is accepting the losses to embrace the new beginnings.

M any times unacknowledged or unreleased feelings keep us stuck in the past. We failed to tell someone we loved them. We failed to be content with what we had. Or we feel that because we did not treat someone right or do something right we don't deserve to move on.

Faith understands life is not about perfection, it is about progress and the lessons learned in between.

Acknowledge the wrong, learn the lesson and move on. Moving on does not mean you love them any less, in fact it celebrates the memories you shared. Moving on allows your loved one to truly rest in peace. In heaven there is no sorrow or pain. Therefore, those left here on earth should rejoice in the peace they now have.

Truth be told mourning is also selfish. Your flesh is having a temper tantrum over what life will be without that person or that thing that you lost. Those in mourning are often heard saying, "how will I go on without so and so?" "what's going to happen to me now?" or "I can't believe she/he/it is gone." After my mother passed I recall saying, "who is going to be proud of me now?" Which was quite ironic considering I had often assumed she didn't care. But it was part of the regret.

We have created soul-ties. Many feel soul-ties are restricted to romantic relationships or sex but soul-ties also refer to other people and things. But how can a loved one, lost house or job be considered a soul-tie? Simply put, as I have said before, because God has determined the season with that person or thing is over and our determination to hold on is therefore deemed ungodly.

Bottom line, he, she, and/or it, is gone. They are not coming back and your refusal to let go is preventing your seasons from changing. A new beginning cannot manifest while we hold on, with such a tight grip, to yesterday.

And Jesus said to them, "Can the friends of the bridegroom mourn as long as the bridegroom is with them? But the days will come when the bridegroom will be taken away from them, and then they will fast. No one puts a piece of unshrunk cloth on an old garment; for the patch pulls away from the garment, and the tear is made worse. Nor do they put new wine into old wineskins, or

> *Many times, our inability to break free from the past is due to mindless attachments we have given it through the words we spoke.*

Finding Faith

else the wineskins break, the wine is spilled, and the wineskins are ruined. But they put new wine into new wineskins, and both are preserved."
—Matthew 9: 15 - 17

Many times, the storms in life, once over, can leave us standing in the middle of what was and what could be afraid to move forward. The fear is based on two things: repeat and the unknown. We are afraid that what happened will happen again and/or we are afraid of not knowing what lies ahead. The turmoil, rubbish, and pain are behind us but the road ahead is not quite clear either, instead it is dark and scary. As humans, we fear what we can't see.

After momma passed and now unemployed for 15 months, I was faced with a decision of returning to my previous job I had before I became unemployed. I spent 15 years there, God told me to leave and go to the new job in social services, why would he want me to go back? My pride would not let me see that sometimes the road to a new beginning does a double loop back before moving forward. I was also ashamed; how could I face all those coworkers that I told I was never coming back. Was I wrong? Did God really tell me to leave the first time and my unemployment was due to my disobedience? Of course not. Fifteen years at one company left me with a false sense of dependency and comfort. God took me away so that I would learn to trust and rely on Him, not a job. My obedience to go back, despite my reservations, fear of ridicule, and pride showed my dependence on God as not only my resource but my source. My obedience also opened the door and enabled God to bless me beyond measure. I was only at that job 5 months and God opened the door for new employment that doubled my salary. Not to mention I had gotten a new place despite my bad credit from the short sale. I also celebrated the launch of my third book. Things were turning around, I was getting double for my trouble, and I was seeing beauty rising from the ashes. But I was walking on egg shells. The wait between leaving one job and transitioning to the new job took two weeks longer than usual. I panicked at the thought of being unemployed again and losing the new townhouse I had just got. How quickly I had forgotten that the Lord had just provided for me through 15 months of unemployment, 2 weeks should have been a breeze.

As I was celebrating my new house, job, and book I couldn't help but be saddened that it all came on the heels of the death of my mother, and the financial hardship of my brother. How could I be happy when she was gone and he was struggling? How could I embrace my new beginning when it meant a season of sorrow for someone else? Survivor's remorse can prevent the will of God from fully manifesting. The same way God ordained and appointed your season of hardship and blessings He does the same for others. Unfortunately, your seasons may not coincide just because you are connected to each other. Just because you are associated does not mean your seasons change simultaneously.

Let Go of the Past

Before you can embrace your new beginning, you must first let go of the past. Letting go of the past requires a few steps. First, acknowledge and release your feelings. Acknowledge your part in what happened or what you took for granted. Release

Finding Faith

your feelings by writing a letter to the person. I wrote a letter to my mother.

Dear Mama,

 I didn't know how your death would affect me. I didn't know the pain, guilt and confusion I would feel. I was angry that you were so tough on me. I was disappointed that you didn't see the effect the molestations left on me. I was upset that you didn't seem to notice I needed you. I needed you to tell me I was beautiful; to hug me when I messed up; to wipe my tears away; or to hold my hand.

 I don't remember you being in the room as I lay on the cold table at the Rape Crisis center and the woman dusted my genitalia for finger prints. I don't recall you being in the court room when I got on the witness stand and pointed to the man who stole my innocence. I was saddened that you didn't notice the weight gain or the change in personality. You didn't see the desperation to love and be loved when I babysat every weekend and tried to have one of my own. I couldn't understand at that time that you did what you knew to do, that you didn't know how to be a good mom; that my suffering triggered guilt of being a bad parent and reminded you of your own history of pain and abuse.

 When you died, I was relieved. Not that you were gone, but that you were free and no longer in pain. I walked in that hospital room and saw the glory of the Lord shining over your body. I couldn't cry, instead I rejoiced knowing you were finally embraced by the love you spent your whole life searching for. Then I was thankful that I was free as well. The anger and hurt no longer mattered. I felt the stone of bitterness and anger over my heart, shatter. My whole countenance changed. I was confused, because how could your death bring me freedom? Then I was filled with regret. I regretted the time that we missed. The realization set in that I no longer had *a mother. I no longer had a safe place or a plan B to fall back on if times got hard. I no longer had a bosom to rest in when I got weary. You wouldn't be here when I finally got married or had my first child; that grandchild you always wanted. You wouldn't be my cheerleader anymore. Who would I make proud now?*

I also felt guilty. How could I move on at your expense? How could your death bring me freedom? How could I be happy without you? But I now realize that motherhood does not end at death, it continues on into eternity. You were unable to rest knowing that I was stuck in guilt and regret. You were unable to enjoy God's presence watching me succumb to sorrow. Even from the grave, you are still my mother. I release you!

Forgive me for the tears and pain I caused with my bad attitude and saying no when I could have said yes. Forgive me for the missed phone calls and not being by your side when God called you home. As you embrace paradise, I embrace my freedom and walk in forgiveness. I release you to rest in heavenly peace. Enter into the joy of the Lord knowing that your baby girl is fine. I am and I will continue in the plans you and God have for me. You are forgiven. Your love was not perfect, but you loved perfectly. Please forgive me. Rest on Sister Girl!

Forever, Your Baby Girl

The letter allowed me to deal with the emotions of my past, the actions I took or failed to take out of anger, and the regret I felt over not knowing her fully and allowing her to be who God created her to be in my life. The letter also ended the torment of the enemy over what should have been said and done.

The beauty of my mother's death is that God honored me. He warned me thus allowing me time to repair our relationship. I was able to care for her and pray for her in her last days.

Finding Faith

He didn't allow her to die at home, sparing me the tragedy of discovering her body. In one act, he healed her and delivered me. In one night, he flooded my mind and heart with good memories to drown out the bad. Before, my anger only allowed me to dwell on the bad recollections of my childhood, but my deliverance allowed me to recover the beauty in her effort to give me what she never had . . . a chance to be better!

Second, forgive yourself. Forgive yourself from any regret, shame, or guilt. Regardless of what happened, you made it through and you can't change what happened. Repent for the wrong you did, accept God's forgiveness, and walk in freedom knowing there is no condemnation in God. The condemnation is a trick of the enemy to keep you stuck dwelling on the past and dwelling on things that you had no control over. Even when you thought you messed up, you were still in God's will. Walking in freedom acknowledges God as Lord of your life. Which brings me to the third step: Accept God's plan.

Accept the Assignment

"For My thoughts are not your thoughts, nor are your ways My ways," says the LORD. "For as the heavens are higher than the earth, so are My ways higher than your ways, and My thoughts than your thoughts."

—Isaiah 55: 8 - 9

God is the alpha and omega, the beginning and the end. Faith dwells in the middle! Faith is between belief and manifestation. If we knew what would happen, how it would happen and when it would happen, we would not need God. Every dream, every talent, and every gift He placed inside of you comes with conditions. Conditions that you don't give up, don't question, and remember His word.

The storm was not supposed to stop you. It was not supposed to make you question your life's path. It was not supposed to rattle your belief system. It was not supposed to make you fear what lies ahead. The storm came to prepare you for what you prayed for. The storm came to teach you how to fully depend on God and surrender to His will. The storm came to show you how to rest in His presence and obtain peace despite turmoil. The storm came to propel you into the greatness that you were created for. The loss of loved ones and valued possessions was simply an indication of the changing of seasons. The storm came to confirm who you are that you may recognize the strength, presence and character of He who is in you.

The storm came that you may know God for yourself. The storm came to provide deeper insight into your purpose. But who told you to stop dreaming? Who told you to stop participating in God's plan? This walk is a partnership between you and God. What you went through was not to punish you or stop you from dreaming. It was to show you that God is the originator and executioner of your dreams. Your faith is strengthened by the storms. It is a mystery to those who don't know God. They don't understand happiness, peace, joy, love,

> *The storm came to test your faith, not in the promise but in He who gave the promise.*

contentment, etc., in times of trouble. Faith is easy when things are going well, but the faith to stand in the storm is the sustenance of our Christian walk. Your faith is your witness to those watching. Those watching from afar, that have seen what you went through, are able to observe the God of restoration through you.

Embrace the new beginning because you deserve it. Sometimes even struggle and lack can become comfortable. Because of your faith, because you did not give up, and because you did not turn your back on God, you deserve it. Because you kept getting back up, because you didn't allow the enemy to defeat you with thoughts of doubt and fear, you deserve it. Because you kept proclaiming the goodness of the Lord, because you kept expecting better to come, you deserve it.

Many Christians believe the cliché "what God has for me is for me," but I have yet to find a scripture to support that in the context in which it is used. As we learned in Chapter 3, unbelief and sin can halt the hand of God. Procrastination and fear can as well. Faith requires us to trust in God, that includes His timing and direction. Just as seasons change in the natural without your permission, so is the same in the spiritual. While the season may come again, we do not know the elements it will bring with it.

> *The storm wasn't meant to last forever, you prolong the next season by refusing to embrace the new beginning.*

Indiana Tuggle

Expect God to Show Up

It's funny how as Christians we expect the trials and tribulations, yet we don't expect for things to get better. We call it pride or arrogance when we see people boasting on the word of the Lord. Or calling them pseudo saints, and proclaiming, "it doesn't take all that," when they spout out scripture. But in order to embrace your new beginning, you have to expect the word to produce fruit in your life. You have to expect God to do what He said He would do; otherwise your suffering was in vain. Otherwise His word is a lie, He is unable to turn things around for our good.

The new beginning actually isn't about you. It's about God. It's about His reputation. Do you honestly think that you walking around living a life of holiness, proclaiming the Lord as your personal savior and sharing your testimony with others can go unnoticed? The reason that doubt and fear has such a tight grip is because you are surrounded by naysayers. I remember when I was unemployed, people were telling me to get a job, any job. But I knew what God had told me, I knew what I wanted, salary and responsibility wise, in my next role and I knew God had given me a season of rest to gain clarity. The words they spoke weighed heavily on my heart and bombarded my thoughts; it fueled my doubt.

> *Faith embraces the new beginning because it doesn't want to miss the move of God. God is time and He controls the season. But that does not mean the season will wait for you.*

Finding Faith

I now understand why God kept telling me to make my circle smaller. The new beginning is so that His word concerning you can come to pass; to prove to the naysayers that the God you serve has not forgotten you and more importantly He is the name above all names. Embrace your new beginning because it's time to sit at the table God has been preparing for you.

Faith embraces its new beginning with joy and pride, because God showed up just like He said He would.

birthday or more than one Christmas gift. Yes, we were poor in both locations, but we had never gone without.

One day my good friend and boyfriend's sister went to stay with her aunt. Her aunt and my mother were close, in that they occasionally did drugs together, so my mother would allow me to spend weeks at a time over at her house with my friend. We both went to the same high school and they actually lived down the street from our school. Other than to go downtown or to the mall for shopping, we never really ventured outside of the projects or our immediate neighborhood. This area on the other side of Sheffield High School was new territory, Southeast Memphis or Parkway Village is what it was called. We would walk approximately two miles, through the neighborhoods to get to school and home every day. I often admired the neighborhood; the manicured lawns, vibrant brick and neutral colors on the exterior, it always looked so safe and peaceful. One day on the way to school during the course of our conversation, I abruptly stated, "I'm going to have a house over here one day." "What?" my friend asked in confusion because my statement came out of nowhere and obviously did not add to the conversation we were having. I repeated, "I'm going to have a house over here one day." "Oh," she said, "Me too." We both smiled and nodded at each other, and jumped back into whatever we were talking about.

That conversation took place in the early 90's. I graduated high school in '95. That summer she, her brother and I, got an apartment together close to the school but on the other side. A few years later her brother and I broke up, I moved out and she and I lost touch. But in 2004, I purchased my first house in that neighborhood. I remember feeling a sense of home as my realtor and I pulled up to the house to take the first viewing. At the closing table, when the closing attorney handed me the keys, as he said congratulations, a small, still voice whispered, "You said it." At first, I paid it no mind, but after I moved in and was walking down my drive way to check the mailbox, I heard it again, "You said it." "What?" I asked, my voice trembling. "You said you would live in this neighborhood." At that moment God reminded me of the conversation I had with my friend, walking through that very neighborhood over 10 years before.

Though I had forgotten the words spoken, my mind, strategically following the instructions given it over 10 years earlier, took steps to make it come to pass. It was no coincidence that the houses I looked at in other neighborhoods did not speak to me. My heart already knew what it was looking for. I had rented a townhouse on the other side of town, yet when it was time to buy I did not like any of the houses in that area. Because I had spoken it, my heart was not going to settle for anything less. That is the power that we possess as believers of Christ.

> *Faith knows that when it opens its mouth, the angels take flight to perform what has been spoken. Our bodies align in agreement unwilling and unable to accept a counterfeit.*

(as it is written, "I have made you a father of many nations") in the presence of Him whom he believed—God, who gives life to the dead and calls those things which do not exist as though they did; who, contrary to *hope, in hope believed, so that he became the father of many nations, according to what was spoken, "So shall your descendants be."*

—*Romans 4: 17-18*

What do you want from God? Is it in His will? Sometimes we can want something from God that's not in His will. I'm not speaking of grandiose dreams, because I'm a firm believer that you can't out dream God. If he placed it in you, He can make it happen. But I'm speaking of coveting the things of others. Do you want what God wants for you or what someone else has? Check your motives and then check the word. Find a scripture that supports what you are praying for and stand on that word. Earlier I discussed my period of unemployment. The scripture I quoted most was Philippians 4:19, "My God shall supply all my needs according to His riches in glory." I kept praying that scripture over and over, one day I got angry at God because I had not gained employment. He responded, "I did what you asked." I stepped back and noticed that though I did not have a job, I had food, gas when I needed it, a roof over my head, etc. Right as He was, and grateful as I was, I needed to find another scripture to obtain what I wanted.

Many Christians often pick up scripture based off what they have heard others say rather than

The word will do what it's supposed to but we are to be sure we are using the right word.

what they specifically need. If you are standing on the word, be sure you are standing on the right word!

Do you have what you want? What are you saying about it? Now don't get me wrong, just because you speak it today does not mean you will have it tomorrow. If that were the case faith would not be necessary. Faith continues to speak the promises and word of God regardless of what today looks like. As I mentioned earlier, faith lies in between belief and manifestation. What are you speaking as you wait? What are you speaking when the enemy attacks your finances, sleep, job, family, friends, etc.? What are you speaking when the dream and your reality are worlds apart?

What God has for you is for you, but the words spoken in the journey can delay its arrival. Not because you prevented the word from going forth, but because you stopped your feet from moving and your hands from working. Faith without works is dead (Hebrews 11:1). Therefore, procrastination and disobedience prevent faith from working. Both are routed in doubt and are a result of negative thinking and speaking. For example, you can't believe God for increase in your business, yet complain about the lack of support and inability to make sales or conjure up new clients. The complaints lead you to thinking that perhaps business is slow

Faith understands that what you say in the process, determines how long the journey to the promise will be.

because the products aren't good and people just don't see value in what you have. Then the negative thinking leads you to stop placing ads on social media or shut down your account all together, you stop going to networking events to meet like-minded people, and just sit at home watching television and eating potato chips. Next your prayer life becomes non-existent because you stopped spending time in the word. Finally, you become frustrated and confused wondering if God has forgotten about you.

God has not forgotten. You forgot! You forgot you said yes. You forgot you told God you would do His will no matter how hard it gets. You forgot He never promised you it would be easy. He never promised you the increase would come overnight. No longer curse in your frustration, what God has already said is blessed. Faith believes the promise even in the face of adversity.

Faith understands that the journey is just as important as the final destination.

Faith knows that the lesson in the journey will be the foundation that keeps the promise going. God knows what He is doing. If he gave it to you overnight, you would not appreciate it. Faith is not validated or moved by the actions of man. Instead, it constantly pursues the presence of God. For in His presence is the clarity and guidance you need. His word says He teaches us to prosper. You cannot be taught if you refuse to come to class. Are you skipping school? I remember when I was in high school, in some classes I would cut and go to the ROTC building and hang out with my friends. Because the tests were always open book, I would show up on test day, pass and repeat the following week. However, to this day I cannot tell you anything I actually learned in those classes. Well, faith comes by hearing, and hearing by the word of God. You have to spend as much time listening to His voice as you do reading His word. Attempting to read the bible in frustration only creates more frustration. Your thoughts are not calm, they are too loud and thus drowning out His voice.

Faith is a product of a consistent relationship with God. Funny how we expect God to be faithful yet we are not faithful to Him.

We cannot do it without Him. Attempting to do so leads to wasted money and time. Your confusion and frustration are a result of your impatience, which is evidence of lack of faith. Nothing is working because you are working alone. Before God will allow you to mess up His name or distort His plan with selfish ambition, He will halt the work of your hands.

Repent and go back to the meeting place. Go back to the presence of God. Schedule him back into your day. Commit to the time you set. Make it happen. Revisit the vision.

"Write the vision and make it plain on tablets, that he

> *Faith does not know the path ahead, but it rests in the one leading.*

may run who reads it"
—Habakkuk 2:2

We all know this scripture and recite it often, myself included. But how many actually write the vision? I used to think vision board parties were a waste of time and effort. However, it is a very powerful thing to do. Writing the vision is an instruction from God and a reminder to you when things don't go as you hoped or the journey seems too much to bear. Which brings me to the next verse in that scripture:

"For the vision is yet for an appointed time; but at the end it will speak, and will not lie. Though it tarries, wait for it; because it will surely come, it will not tarry."
–Habakkuk 2:3

We seem to stop at verse 2, but it's in verse 3 that we discover that the vision will take time! Wait, you mean it's not going to happen overnight? There are some very significant points I need to point out in this scripture:

1. The vision is for an appointed time. Writing the vision is not for immediate gratification or success. It is an act of acknowledging the voice of God in you and heeding His instructions. God has a set time in which it will come to pass.

2. At the end it will speak and will not lie. The vision will speak to you! As you go, it is that written vision that will confirm your direction. If you are confused about which way to go it is because you have not written the vision.

3. Though it tarries, wait for it. It's going to take time. Delay does not mean denial nor does it mean you need to change courses. The process, though not written, is essential to the vision.

4. It will surely come, it will not tarry. I know you are confused here. The word just said "though it tarries." But this is not a conflict. It is reassurance that if you stick to the plan, it will happen. We tend to confuse "wait" with doing nothing. Which, as I said earlier, if you do nothing, nothing will happen. Wait means to serve. You are to be serving, and as you do so, the vision will unfold before your eyes.

> *Doubt and fear are signs that the gate to our hearts and minds are left unguarded.*

Did you write the vision? I love to journal. I keep a journal of my quiet time with God. I keep a journal of all the words spoken over me rather through others or direct communication from God. I also keep a journal of the things I want for my business. When I get frustrated I pull out the journal of words spoken over me so that I can be reminded of God's promises. When things are not going the way that I hoped and I'm all stressed out, I pull out the business journal and see if I am following the vision that I wrote and was given to me. That latter part of Habakkuk 2:2, "that he may run who reads it," is for you. You must read it whenever it is necessary to remind you of the plan. Stay the course. Stay in His presence.

Our refuge, strength, and faith are in God's presence. It is only when we have allowed trials and circumstances to keep us from praying and reading His word that doubt and fear come in. Listening to sermons and music cannot replace quality time with God. He is waiting to sup with you, to commune with you in your secret place. It is the plan of the enemy to keep you from Him. Peace is in His presence. Joy is in His presence. Guidance is in His presence. He cannot guide you if you don't come to Him to hear his command. The written vision is the destination, but the directions to get there are given in His presence. Faith trusts that it is on the right path regardless of the condition of the road. Anxiety and frustration are not of God, they are indicative of weakened faith. Writing the vision is an understanding of your assignment. Allow God to lead you to the open doors, divine connections and the appointed time.

Your impatience and limited eyesight are preventing you from seeing God working and His strategies unfolding.

But put on the Lord Jesus Christ and make no provision for the flesh to fulfill its lust.

—Romans 13:14

Faith rests in knowing: knowing that God is pleased, knowing that you are in His will, knowing that obedience is the key, knowing that God is with you and knowing God will not allow you to fail.

You put on the Lord by praying, studying, meditating, and acknowledging Him in all you do. Doing so consistently gives you the power to deny the flesh. The flesh wants to be lazy. The flesh wants to procrastinate. The flesh wants to give up. The flesh focuses on materialistic desires of money, things and people. The flesh believes these things are the key to success. God is the key. He is the connection. He is all you need. Once you realize that and stay in consistent communication, God can work and you will stop seeking the help of others. To stop communicating says that you don't need God. Faith knows that purpose is a partnership between you and God. You fight the doubt, validation seeking, insecurities, fear, etc., by continuing to seek God.

Faith is a daily "Yes" to God when your flesh is determined to say no.

Restore your commitment. Say "Yes" again! When you are weary in well-doing, say, "YES, Lord." When things are not working out right, say, "YES, Lord." When things seem to be going in the wrong direction, say, "YES, Lord." When chaos and anxiety seem to take over, say, "YES, Lord." When lack appears to rise, say, "YES, Lord."

Yes, is a reminder and acknowledgment of the will of God. It is a decision to choose God despite present circumstances. Yes, activates your faith, rejuvenates your spirit, and energizes you to continue. Yes, gives focus to the things of God. Yes, is a reminder that God is in control when you get lost in daily struggles. Yes, is a reminder that God's plan for your life is already set when you forget your purpose and assignment. Don't forget you said yes!

Watch What You Say

Be mindful of the words you speak. What you speak in frustration today can impact the day you see tomorrow. You see what you say, so speak what you want. We quote scripture and appear holy to others but we cannot fool God.

Brood of vipers! How can you, being evil speak good things? For out of the abundance of the heart the mouth speaks. A good man out of the good treasure of his heart brings forth good things, and an evil man out of the evil treasure brings forth evil things. But I say to you that for every idle word men may speak, they will give an account of it in the day of judgment. For by your words you will be justified, and by your words you will be condemned.

—*Matthew 12: 34-37*

> *Faith speaks the word and awaits its manifestation.*

The heart cannot lie. Check your motives. Your needs have tainted the intent of your purpose. Your lips speak loosely out of lack in a fleshly pursuit of an earthly reward for a Godly assignment. Walking by faith, as the word commands, requires knowledge of God's character and how He moves. In the book of

Matthew when God told Peter to get out of the boat and come to Him, Peter did not sink because God was not able to keep him from drowning. Peter sank because he took his eyes off God and placed them on his own abilities. When we speak the word, we take ourselves and our limited abilities out of the equation and ignite the power, authority, and ability of God. Faith recognizes that we are the clay, mere vessels, and God is the potter. Speaking the word, relinquishes our own will for His will. When Jesus cried out in the garden knowing his betrayal was near, "Father, if it is Your will, take this cup away from Me; nevertheless, not My will but Yours be done." (Luke 22:42), it helped me understand the plight of purpose. It will be painful. You will endure great trials and tribulations. Pain causes the flesh to speak in haste to end its suffering. But even Jesus had to come to Himself! He recognized it wasn't about Him. He recognized He accepted the assignment. He recognized that God was still in control. The dying of His flesh on that cross allowed us to see the depth of His love and the sacrifice required to truly walk by faith. Walking by faith requires the fear of the Lord. We have to be willing to sacrifice, that which is near and dear to our heart to walk in fear (reverence and sole obedience to His command) of the Lord.

Watch what you say! I know it's uncomfortable. I know it doesn't feel good. God is not moved by your tears. He did not accept the invitation to your pity party. Responding to the hurt, though normal, don't stay there. As my mother would say, "Snap out of it," pull yourself together, remember you said YES and speak the word. God never said we had to memorize every scripture in the bible. Find one or two that pertains to what you are going through, stand firm in them, and watch God.

Finding Faith

And we know that all things work together for good to those who love God, to those who are called according to His purpose.

—Romans 8:28

Faith is not about perfection, it is about confidence that God will perform that which He said He would do. You don't have to look for faith, it is not hard to find . . . Just Look Up!

ABOUT THE AUTHOR

In addition to being an author, Indiana is also an inspirational speaker, life and writing coach and the CEO of Victory Publishing Co. A native of Memphis, TN and educated in Social Work (BSW), Public Administration (MPC) and Counseling (MPC), Indiana hopes her life experiences and faith will inspire others to live courageously and boldly in pursuit of their God-given purpose as well as increase their relationship with Christ.

Through her books, teaching, speaking, coaching and business endeavors she helps women heal from past trauma, find their identity in Christ, and uncover their purpose in their pain. She also assists aspiring writers in writing and publishing their testimonies to draw others to Christ.

Other Titles by Indiana:

Stop Asking Why Are You Single-A journey towards healing and contentment in Christ journeys how Indiana healed from past traumas of molestation, domestic violence, poverty, poor relationships and low self-esteem, learned how to forgive and found her happiness in Christ.

Saved, Single & Frustrated-A guide to unleash the best in you while you wait provides singles with Christian advice to guide them through the single season in how to release the frustration, recognize their worth, break soul-ties, set standards in dating, examine why they want to be married, etc while enjoying life and waiting for their spouse.

Awaken the Dream-90-Day Devotional provides encouragement and motivation to those struggling to find and pursue their dreams and purpose. Life happens but we must never give up.

Learn more about her and her books at www.indianatuggle.com. For information on her business endeavors visit www.victorypublishingco.com

ACKNOWLEDGEMENTS

To my Tuggle and Powerhouse family, friends, and co-workers thank you for being the supportive network I need to keep my dreams alive. You never allow me to give up and always pray me through every situation. I love you dearly and am eternally grateful for the love you continue to show.

To my Lord and Savior Jesus Christ you never cease to amaze me. Thank you for choosing me!

A WORD FROM THE AUTHOR

Keep Going

I know it is hard and I know it may seem that the enemy is throwing everything your way but keep going. One day you too will look back and recognize the lessons of faith that made you the man or woman you were meant to be. Keep reading, keep praying, keep standing, and never forget the promises God made. Surround yourself with other believers and stay connected to a bible-based church. Know that you are not alone. Faith is not about perfection, it is about trust. Keep Going, greatness awaits you on the other side!

www.ingramcontent.com/pod-product-compliance
Lightning Source LLC
Chambersburg PA
CBHW070609010526
44118CB00012B/1478